T0205151

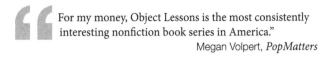

For my money, Object Lessons is the most consistently interesting nonfiction book series in America."

Megan Volpert, *PopMatters*

Besides being beautiful little hand-sized objects themselves, showcasing exceptional writing, the wonder of these books is that they exist at all. . . . Uniformly excellent, engaging, thought-provoking, and informative."

Jennifer Bort Yacovissi,
Washington Independent Review of Books

. . . edifying and entertaining . . . perfect for slipping in a pocket and pulling out when life is on hold."

Sarah Murdoch, *Toronto Star*

[W]itty, thought-provoking, and poetic. . . . These little books are a page-flipper's dream."

John Timpane, *The Philadelphia Inquirer*

Though short, at roughly 25,000 words apiece, these books are anything but slight."

Marina Benjamin, *New Statesman*

OBJECT LESSONS

A book series about the hidden lives of ordinary things.

Series Editors:

Ian Bogost and Christopher Schaberg

Advisory Board:

Sara Ahmed, Jane Bennett, Jeffrey Jerome Cohen, Johanna Drucker, Raiford Guins, Graham Harman, renée hoogland, Pam Houston, Eileen Joy, Douglas Kahn, Daniel Miller, Esther Milne, Timothy Morton, Kathleen Stewart, Nigel Thrift, Rob Walker, Michele White

In association with

BOOKS IN THE SERIES

office

SHEILA LIMING

BLOOMSBURY ACADEMIC
NEW YORK • LONDON • OXFORD • NEW DELHI • SYDNEY

BLOOMSBURY ACADEMIC
Bloomsbury Publishing Inc
1385 Broadway, New York, NY 10018, USA
50 Bedford Square, London, WC1B 3DP, UK

First published in the United States of America 2020

Cover design: Alice Marwick

For legal purposes the Acknowledgments on p. 117 constitute an extension of this copyright page.

Library of Congress Cataloging-in-Publication Data
Names: Liming, Sheila, author.
Title: Office / Sheila Liming.
Description: New York: Bloomsbury Academic, 2020. | Series: Object lessons | Includes
bibliographical references and index. | Summary: "On the cultural significance of the office-as
an icon, as a space, and as a vanishing species in the 21st century"– Provided by publisher.
Identifiers: LCCN 2020014180 | ISBN 9781501348679 (paperback) | ISBN 9781501348693 (pdf)
| ISBN 9781501348686 (ebook)
Subjects: LCSH: Offices–Social aspects.
Classification: LCC HD1393.55 .L55 2020 | DDC 306.3/6–dc23
LC record available at https://lccn.loc.gov/2020014180

ISBN: PB: 978-1-5013-4867-9
ePDF: 978-1-5013-4869-3
eBook: 978-1-5013-4868-6

Series: Object Lessons

Typeset by Deanta Global Publishing Services, Chennai, India
Printed and bound in the United States of America

To find out more about our authors and books visit www.bloomsbury.com and sign up
for our newsletters.

To my father, Jim Liming,
in recognition of his fifty years at the office.

CONTENTS

FIGURES

INTRODUCTION

All the World's an Office

Perched high atop a multistory building on the Carnegie Mellon University campus in Pittsburgh, there sits an office. *Whose* office is unclear, since a rotating cast of companies—everything from tech startups to local non-profit organizations—have occupied it over the years. And just like its tenants, its physical features are subject to alteration and change: walls get moved around, new lighting schemes are born and then dispensed with, the temperature fluctuates, and furniture arrangements come and go. All of these modifications, though, are part of the plan. This is the Robert L. Preger Intelligent Workplace, which Carnegie Mellon's School of Architecture maintains as a "living laboratory" of workplace design, a sort of testing ground for office functionality. Its creator, Professor Volker Hartkopf, now Emeritus at Carnegie Mellon, adapts the language of performance in his attempts to describe it, calling it "a stage, like a theater, on top of which you can play out any organizational requirement."[1]

The Preger Intelligent Workplace has been around for more than a decade, but its immediate effects are minimal. Elsewhere at Carnegie Mellon, for instance, one still encounters the trappings of a more traditional style of office life, including nonadjustable thermostats, insipid overhead lighting and, yes, cubicles. I myself occupied one of them—in a basement—for years. There, I grew accustomed to the electrical fizz and splutter that results from malfunctioning fluorescent tubes. I didn't know that, just down the way, workers were being treated to "sunflower" style lights that track the movement of the sun and adjust and dim accordingly. If I had, I surely would have been jealous.

In labeling his Intelligent Workplace office a "stage," Hartkopf calls attention to the link between offices and ideas of *performance*. As the primary site of work in the postmodern era, the office has lent a definite, physical shape to the performance of less physical forms of work. Its proliferation in the early twentieth century coincided with the rise of jobs that emphasized the importance of brains over brawn—jobs once labeled "white collar," since performing them didn't require getting one's hands dirty (and so could be done while wearing a white, collared dress shirt). The idea was that an office was where one went to work with their brain, while the factory or the farm placed demands upon one's body.

The novelist Upton Sinclair, who achieved fame when he exposed the evils of industrialized meat production in *The Jungle* (1916), drew attention to the term "white collar" in a separate work published in 1919, during an era that saw that expansion of office work as industrialization made certain forms of physical labor redundant. The white-collar office-dweller, in Sinclair's view, stood in apparent opposition to the manual laborer and, thus, to labor organizing efforts as well.

> It is a fact with which every union workingman is familiar, that his most bitter despisers are the petty underlings of the business world, the poor office-clerks, who are often the worst exploited of proletarians, but who, because they are allowed to wear a white collar, and to work in the office with the boss, regard themselves as members of the capitalist class.[2]

Sinclair's point is that office workers view themselves as separate, but that they are in fact still "poor underlings," just like their blue-collar counterparts.

When Sinclair was writing in the early decades of the 1900s, office work was ascendant, much like the office itself. A growing number of workers across the globe were adjusting to the routines of office life and during the Depression, while farmers weathered the effects of the Dust Bowl and other catastrophes (both natural and otherwise), rates of white-collar office employment continued to grow. Today, though, the office's star appears to be in decline. Following a trend that first took hold in the 1970s, more and more white-collar workers today are permitted and, in some cases, *expected* to do their jobs remotely—either from home, while traveling, or else from ad hoc spaces like coffee shops. A 2017 Gallup poll, for instance, puts the number of remotely laboring American workers at 43 percent.[3]

Hartkopf and his team's attempts to reimagine core aspects of office life thus appear aspirational in many respects, but they also signal growing concern about the future of these spaces. A number of companies struggling to find ways to get workers *into* the office, for instance, have turned to incentivizing attendance. Google made waves in the early 2000s with the establishment of its corporate "campuses," which tried to inject collegiate-style levity into the modern workplace via features like smoothie machines and beanbag chairs. Meanwhile, other companies were countering Google's carrot-like approach with new takes on the proverbial stick: Yahoo CEO Melissa Mayer announced a controversial ban on telecommuting in 2013, ordering the company's employees back to the office.[4] At the time, Mayer cited concerns for productivity and, indeed, some studies have shown that stay-at-home workers tend to get less done. But Mayer's decision struck many as a feeble attempt to erect a crude dam in the face of a swelling tide.

Your Office, My Office

This book is an attempt to reckon with the many meanings of the office, as well as its history and its future, in the face of what looks and feels like a moment of flux and, possibly, decline. It argues for particular interpretations of the many, nested factors that have contributed to that decline even as it acknowledges the deeply personal attachments that people have to their offices, and the quality of those attachments moving forward. As such, it is does not seek to provide a comprehensive history of offices and office spaces; rather, it offers an extended contemplation on the role that they have played in culture, in many people's personal lives and, to a certain extent, in my own.

I grew up in the era of Take Our Daughters to Work Day, an annual event launched in the mid-1990s by the Ms. Foundation (with support from *Ms.* magazine founder and feminist icon, Gloria Steinem) that, in recent decades, has expanded and has come be known as Take Our Daughters and Sons to Work Day. My parents both worked in offices—my father at a bank and my mother at a community college—and, when I was twelve, I paid a visit to their respective places of work under the auspices of that annual holiday. My mother's office struck me as providing a more legible working environment than my father's; since she taught at the community college, her personal office, and the wider departmental facilities that enveloped it, seemed to logically serve as a home base for her teaching duties. At my father's office, though, I struggled to discern what the individual spaces—let alone the people inside of them—were actually for, since they all seemed more or less uniform in appearance. All the rooms (or ad hoc spaces formed by partition walls, like his own) contained the same things, with all of the people inside appearing identically preoccupied.

For a middle-schooler like myself, Take Your Daughter to Work Day provided first and foremost a day to skip school. But it also impressed upon me the likelihood that an office would form an inevitable part of my own future someday, almost regardless of the specifics of my career choices. These visits also showed me a different side of my parents: I witnessed their professional interactions, which differed sharply from those shaped by our shared domestic environs, and began to see how their office spaces might have given rise to them. I saw how, for both my mom and my dad, their offices gestured in faint, unobtrusive ways toward a personality formed by a life lived *outside* of work, but likewise how that personality was leveraged to forge connections and meanings *inside* of work. My mom's office, for instance, included a giant stuffed cow and a comical array of novelty condoms (she specialized in obstetrics and gynecology, and that included STIs), while my dad's featured prints of the mountains to which he devoted so many of his weekends. And, of course, they both had photos of my sister and me displayed on their desks.

Now in my mid-thirties, I've had a number of offices of my own over the years. My very first was a converted supply closet with a window that looked, dispiritingly enough, onto an *actual* supply closet. It was followed by a couple of cubicles, then some shared room-like accommodations, then at last a room of one's—my—own when I landed my first job as a professor. But there's one thing that all these offices of mine have had in common: they've all been in basements, every single one of them. There are many reasons for this, I think, including the fact that I still rank among the younger and more junior members of my profession, but there are also subtler and more complex forces at work that serve to keep me basement-bound, much like the *X-Files*' Mulder and Scully, two of my childhood heroes.

One of those factors stems from the lack of prestige associated with my discipline, English. At my university, for instance, engineering and STEM disciplines receive pride of place with facilities to match, whereas my own department is located in the oldest building on campus. I don't mind, though, because that leaves it richly layered with history and with meaning. On the inside of my office closet, one can find a clipping taken from a 1948 edition of the student paper. Elsewhere, previous occupants have left their marks, with initials cropping up on walls and furniture. Similarly, a colleague who teaches at Dartmouth showed me a log posted on the inside of her office door listing all of the previous occupants and stretching back more than a hundred years. For me, at least, there is comfort to be found in such minor legacies of use and habitation. I like to know that the work I am doing forms yet another link on a long chain extending decades beyond my own experience and understanding. For one, it makes the work easier to do—others have done it already, after all; on the other hand, it also bequeaths the significance of tradition.

This book is born from a desire to wrestle with both office traditions and with traditional offices, but it also confronts their veritable inverse in the form of demands for innovation. As the initial example of the Preger Intelligent Workplace illustrates, the office has been a battleground for dreams of bureaucratic progress, and thus likewise for manipulation. Changes to the office over the years have been largely implemented with the goal of changing *workers*— their habits, their interactions and, above all, their output. What might seem, at first glance, like cosmetic alterations or a mere shifting of furniture often serves to conceal a more human-centered agenda. And this is where the darker side of Hartkopf's use of the phrase "living laboratory" suddenly comes to the fore: what, or who, is being experimented on here, and to what end?

The Return of Obsolescence

In a 1968 children's book called *Busy Office, Busy People*, young readers are introduced to the fictional Star Shoe Company and to the human beings who see to operations at its corporate headquarters. "There are all kinds of offices, big and small," it informs its readers, with the help of illustrations that show workers (mostly women) positioned behind all sorts of desks located in different settings. It then asks the question, "What would happen if there were no offices?", prompting readers to imagine the resulting chaos of a world where information doesn't get filed and organized and profit isn't measured and counted. "That's why we need more office workers and more machines," it concludes, somewhat artlessly. Except that the workers, it turns out, are less important than the machines: "Machines work faster than people. Office workers must learn to use them."[5]

Busy Office, Busy People responds to the kinds of fears about automation that sprouted to life in the 1950s and were epidemic by the 1960s. Though, just two years earlier, a federal Commission on Technology, Automation, and Economic Progress had tried to waylay some of those fears by insisting that automation was not to blame for job losses, it nonetheless admitted that new machines were "a major factor in the displacement and temporary unemployment of particular workers."[6] At the same time, the commission pointed out that most of the jobs being lost were in the blue-collar sector, while white-collar work—that is, the work of information management and associated forms of machine-*tending*—was projected to be on the rise. Hence *Busy Office, Busy People*'s propagandistic recruiting calls. The world of the office, which reached its zenith in mid-century America, had redefined the very idea of work, and it needed to flesh out its ranks.

As offices became normal during these decades, culture began to offer up more and more images of them, creating a steady diet of aestheticized, office-centered stories to flatter these workers' real-life experiences. *The Mary Tyler Moore Show* in the 1970s ushered in an explosion of office sitcoms following in the 1980s and 1990s and laid the groundwork for more contemporary favorites like *The Office* and *Silicon Valley*. Meanwhile, movies like *Nine to Five*

FIGURE 1 Page from the children's book *Busy Office, Busy People* (1968) by Jene Barr, with illustrations by Charles Lynch III.

(1980) and *Working Girl* (1988), following in *Mary Tyler Moore*'s footsteps, emphasized the experiences of women, in particular, in deference to rising statistics about female office workers. These shows and films formed an alternative core to American entertainment: they focused on work, not the home, and work almost always now included offices.

It makes sense, then, that the sunset concluding the golden age of the office ought to come with its own suite of cultural texts and examples, and it has. Part of my efforts in this book involve surveying those examples to see what clues they may offer for visions of life *after* the office. As *Busy Office, Busy People* tries to show, it's hard to imagine a world without offices—without, that is, the physical enclosures and conceptual containers that don't just make white-collar, intellectual, or creative work happen but, in fact, help us to recognize it in the first place. One might as well imagine a world without churches, without schools and classrooms, without grocery stores (all of which, like offices, now exist online in one form or another).

That end of the office has been a long time in coming, though. The aptly named Microsoft Office suite—a bundle of productivity applications designed to facilitate the work of the modern office—debuted in 1988, promising to provide a software-based, mobile office. In doing so, it subsumed a variety of common office machines and tasks, including adding machines (through Excel), word processing equipment (through Word), and even the typography and graphic design tools used in advertising (through PowerPoint). Today, its updated moniker, Office 365, provides cloud-based access to these tools and more on a subscription basis and is used by over one billion people worldwide. Our computers are our offices; who needs offices?

This book is my attempt to answer that question and to show that, in fact, most people still *want* offices, even if they don't necessarily need them. What's more, that enduring spirit of want is, to me, just as compelling as the history that inspired it. Despite the annoyances and suffering they have caused us—the broken copiers, the stultifying cubicles, the interpersonal dramas—many of us, it's clear, still desire the essential components of an office working environment, to the extent that some of us are even willing to pay for it. This idea of paying to make the work of getting paid more pleasurable is one that I develop in pieces throughout the book for, in it, there are to be found some disturbing hints about the future of the office.

At heart, though, this book seeks to trouble and complicate even as it takes the form of an homage, paying tribute to the places and people and things that have historically made work *work*, and even those that might have made it more difficult along the way. Built into that discussion is an assortment of subjects (bosses and secretaries and salespeople) and objects (bankers' lamps and swivel chairs and paperweights) alike, as well as the buildings that have held and housed them over the years. They are all part of the big, sprawling museum that is now the office, which has nurtured the work of the mind for generations and—in mutated form, perhaps—cannot help but continue to do so.

1 THE OFFICE AS SPACE

Offices of Antiquity

We know them when we see them. A spirit of similitude and blandness tends to preside over each, whether we're talking about a maze of cubicles or an executive's suite with mahogany paneling and a view of the city skyline. We know what is supposed to happen in these spaces, too: work. Often, it's a type of work that could be performed almost anywhere else, except that custom has decreed that it take place here, within the physical confines of what is known as an *office*.

Above all else, an office means a space. This, at least, is the prevailing contemporary definition of the term. It's one that was hundreds of years in the making, though. The word *office*, which descends from the Latin *oficium*, originally referred to a position or post that came with certain responsibilities (as in the phrase "to hold public office"). It was these metaphorical spaces, or else the people who occupied them, that formed the beginnings of the word. Over the centuries, though, a kind of transubstantiation occurred, and an office became first and foremost a *thing*, a space that could be physically experienced and also inhabited. What has remained consistent throughout its etymological history, though, is the way the word *office* has been used to call attention to conditions of separation. In being elected to a public office, a person becomes separated and distinguished from the masses, who are his constituents. In a similar way, the space of the office, regardless of its physical particularities, tends to denote something that has been set aside, a space *apart*. But apart from what exactly?

The origins of the idea begin simply enough, with the word *office* designating a space for work that existed indoors and, thus, stood apart from the kinds of work taking place outside. Nikil Saval points to the middle of the nineteenth century, explaining that offices developed during that era in order to accommodate new types of work. Because of its newness, that work was initially deemed "unnatural"[1] and characterized by its distance *from* nature. But, as a space, the office has a long history that stretches all the way back to the days of religious enclaves, with medieval scribes arguably serving as some of the first office workers. For example, Herman of Tournai was a twelfth-century abbot who famously chronicled life at his medieval Flemish monastery, describing scenes that would be at home in any modern-day office. Among them is his account of "the cloister," where one might see "more than twelve young monks sitting in chairs in front of small tables and silently writing careful and skillful compositions."[2] Here,

Herman is talking about cloister carrels, individual desks that were designed to accommodate the scribes' work and which would have been arranged within a larger setting known as a scriptorium, or writing house. Medieval scribes toiled away inside these early, office-like spaces, producing handwritten copies of sacred manuscripts.

Scriptoria and chapter houses emerged so that resources—including shelter, heat, and materials like vellum and ink—might be jointly shared among laborers, which included monks but also, sometimes, professional scribes. For this reason, scriptoria became a common feature of cenobitic monasteries, which placed an emphasis on community life as opposed to eremitic (or "hermit") traditions. Meanwhile, other religious orders throughout the medieval world maintained that individual *cells* were best for study and clerical work. Famous examples of monastic cells include Skellig Michael, a Gaelic Christian monastery that was founded between the sixth and eighth centuries on an austere island located off the coast of Ireland (and seen recently in the newest spate of *Star Wars* films). Monks at Skellig Michael lived inside of beehive-shaped huts known as clocháns, which provided only meager protection from the punishing weather. These types of cells emblematized the medieval cleric's lifestyle, which was supposed to have been stripped of luxuries and instead organized around work and study. And because *clerk*, the word used to describe most office workers starting in the nineteenth century, is etymologically fused with the word *cleric*, monks have earned a reputation as the founders—or patron saints, if you will—of the modern-day office.

In 1975, for instance, Xerox launched a popular advertising campaign that featured a lovable, office-dwelling figure known as "Brother Dominic." In the commercial that debuted in July of that same year, an appropriately tonsured Brother Dominic appears slaving away inside his medieval scriptorium. He is seated at his cloister carrel and preparing his copies by candlelight. Gregorian-style chanting forms the soundtrack to his labor, which he eventually presents to his abbot, only to be told that he must produce "500 more sets." Fortunately for Brother Dominic, a hole in the space-time continuum grants him admission to the twentieth century; he is transported to a brightly lit, modern office where a new copying device known as the Xerox 9200 Duplicating System promptly produces the required sets for him. Brother Dominic then returns to his medieval enclave and delivers the sets to his delighted abbot-boss, who issues the campaign's catchphrase: "It's a miracle!"[3]

In the commercial, Brother Dominic acts as a kind of conduit between the *clerics* of medieval Europe and the *clerks* of today. The work that he does inside the scriptorium enables his seamless entrance into the space of the twentieth-century office. Candlelight in the first gets swapped for overhead neon in the second, but these spaces appear nonetheless related to each other. Both, for example, appear defined by a similar set of conditions and restraints, including the employee-supervisor relationship and the occurrence of highly repetitive, tedious labor. Brother Dominic's discovery of a time-saving shortcut for his work maps the sort of anxieties that haunt the modern-day office—namely, the concern for efficiency and speed—onto a historically analogous workspace. As a result, in the Xerox commercial, contemporary bureaucrats and office workers are encouraged to see themselves and their own office spaces as not just historically relevant but as mythic, even. Never mind the fact that illiteracy was the norm throughout medieval Europe, or that monks actually formed part a privileged minority. The Xerox commercial's message is one of camaraderie: all of us modern office workers are the living descendants of Brother Dominic.

The Nineteenth-Century Occupation of the Office

Though it had existed in some form for centuries, the office rose to prominence as a space during the nineteenth century. At least, this is what nineteenth-century literature—brimming with offices and office-dwelling characters—would have you believe. Herman Melville is responsible for crafting one of the more famous exemplars of this tradition in the form of Bartleby the Scrivener, an irritable office worker who stars in the 1853 short story of the same name. Offices and office workers were not the most popular literary subjects when Melville's story was first published,[4] but they were both ascendant species that would, in time, come to define much of the dominant culture.

Previously, in 1841, for instance, the poet and essayist Ralph Waldo Emerson had observed that one's "installment" within an office located in an urban setting was already being viewed as the new standard for both work and success in America. What bothered Emerson was the way offices appeared tied to visions of lifelong career stability. American men were being judged by their abilities to acquire a place in an office and to achieve that level of stability, which Emerson saw as having a ruinous effect on the national psyche. "If the finest genius studies at one of our colleges and is not installed in an office within one year afterwards in the cities or suburbs of Boston or New York, it seems . . . that he is right in being disheartened and in complaining the rest of his life," Emerson explains in his famous essay "Self-Reliance." Yet Emerson argues that the enterprising young man who succeeds in rebounding from failure and in trying his hand at a variety of careers "is worth a hundred of these city dolls."[5] The suggestion is that office workers are more or less all the same, and that a nation comprised of clerks therefore cannot help but become a nation of followers.

One of the most famous and best-selling works of nineteenth-century American literature, for instance, actually *begins* in an office. Few readers of Nathaniel Hawthorne's *The Scarlet Letter* (1850), though, have probably noticed this fact. Hawthorne opens his historical novel, the bulk of which is set in the Massachusetts Bay Colony of the 1600s, with reflections upon the years that he spent working as a customs agent in Salem, Massachusetts. And here, just as in Herman of Tournai's accounts of life within his medieval abbey, are familiar descriptions of office space and office work.

> [O]n ascending the steps, you would discern—in the entry, if it were summer time, or in their appropriate rooms, if wintry or inclement weather—a row of venerable figures, sitting in old-fashioned chairs, which were tipped on their hind legs back against the wall. Oftentimes they were asleep, but occasionally might be heard talking together . . . with that lack of energy that distinguishes . . . all other human beings who depend for subsistence . . . on monopolized labor, on anything but their own independent exertions.[6]

Office work during the nineteenth century had yet to be revolutionized by the Taylorist insistence on efficiency and speed (that would come later, in the twentieth century). That is why, instead of haste, we get lassitude in Hawthorne's descriptions of the office environment, a situation that fueled Emerson's worries about the future of the American psyche.

The space of the office, as both Emerson and Hawthorne present it in their writings from this era, inspired not productive or creative labor but, rather, lethargy. It was a space populated by the somnambulant and the idle, where nothing ever got invented or created or done but, merely, half-heartedly managed or arranged or overseen. This idea appears to have been well established by the midpoint of the nineteenth century, making Melville's story "Bartleby, the Scrivener" look more like a famous reiteration than a point of origin. Melville's story takes place in an office, but that office proves to be more than just a setting: it is a physical reflection of its occupants' aspirations and mentalities. It lacks, for instance, for a view. "Owing to the great height of the surrounding buildings" of New York City's Wall Street, and given its position on the second floor, the windows in Melville's narrator's office look out upon an industrial air shaft at one end and upon a neighboring building's brick façade at the other.[7] These physical details conspire to create an atmosphere of claustrophobia and futility. Melville's characters, meanwhile, enact those feelings and display an increasing reluctance to do their work, which involves the copying of legal documents and so is essentially nonproductive. Two of the office's employees turn varyingly to drink, "their fits relieving each other like guards," while Bartleby himself starves and wastes away after repeatedly declaring that he would "prefer not to" do his work.[8]

Bartleby's inertia in this story is as symbolic as it is symptomatic, though. The nineteenth-century rise of the office corresponded, perplexingly enough, with another trend: the decline in the number of hours actually spent working. This is according to the labor historian Benjamin Kline Hunnicutt, who explains that, from the beginnings of the nineteenth century, and lasting up until the start of the twentieth, "working hours in America were gradually reduced . . . and this is true for most modern industrial nations."[9] That the idea of the office was ascendant even as work itself appeared descendant might seem like paradox but, in fact, the first is a direct expression of the second. Offices looked like spaces of idleness, not work, for the very reason that *most* work was still taking place elsewhere, either out of doors or else in factories and manufacturing centers.

So great was the need to see the office as a space unto itself and thus *apart*, that nineteenth-century factories, when they included offices for the housing of bosses or superiors, went to great lengths to separate them both physically and architecturally from those larger working arenas. We see this kind of separation, for instance, in the English novelist Elizabeth Gaskell's *North and South* (1855), which dramatically captures the encroachment of industrialization on life in mid-nineteenth-century England. Gaskell's protagonist, Margaret Hale, upon her first visit to the sprawling Malborough Mills, observes

a great oblong yard, on one side of which were offices for the transaction of business; on the opposite, an immense many-windowed mill, whence proceeded the continual clank of machinery and the long groaning roar of the steam-engine, enough to deafen those who lived within the enclosure.[10]

Margaret notes how the boss' offices at Marlborough Mills are positioned at a safe distance away from the actual work of manufacturing. That distance, in Gaskell's novel, proves to be at once symbolic and practical; Bessy Higgins, a millworker whom Margaret later befriends, ends up dying of byssinosis, which results from the inhaling of dust from cotton weaving.

In order to be recognized *as* work, then, clerical labor during the nineteenth century had to be contextualized and sanctioned with the help of dedicated physical space. And because it housed a more desirable kind of middle-class labor, it also needed to be protected.

The Modern, Organized Office

The idea of office work gradually took hold and became a more acceptable and likely expression of human labor during the nineteenth century. As it did, the office underwent a transformation, shifting away from its identity as a space of lethargy and waste and toward its twentieth-century incarnation as a space of efficiency and production. One symptom of this transformation was that the office became more recognizable *as* a space; it began to develop a set of hallmarks and characteristics that would, decades later, ripen into full-blown clichés (think water-cooler talk and office pranks).

At the heart of the modern office space, though, was an insistence upon organization. Offices became showrooms and testing grounds for new technologies that promised to revolutionize modern living by making information and resources more accessible. For instance, the National Fire Insurance Company, in a corporate history that it published in 1897, describes its newly built headquarters in Hartford, Connecticut, in lavish, uncompromising detail. In particular, it mentions how the newly occupied offices included "steel cases with rolling shuttered fronts" that "are so accessible and conveniently arranged that any paper desired can be produced at a moment's notice"—and because this is a fire insurance company we're talking about, the cases were also guaranteed to be "fireproof."[11]

A photographic plate accompanying these descriptions shows what the company's new Hartford offices looked like when they were built in 1893. Like many others at the time, they featured an open floor plan composed of individual wooden desks, not unlike a medieval scriptorium. The main floor was surrounded on all sides by walls containing the aforementioned steel cases. On one side of the room, a rolling ladder provided access to the upper shelves of the cases, which loomed some twenty feet off the ground. And whereas Melville's Bartleby had, forty years before, labored amid a windowless gloom, the National Fire Insurance Company offices were designed so as to appear "flooded with light from the roof down through the wells on each floor." Such improvements were in keeping with the company's image and with its desire to create "a working office for a working Company."[12]

Window light and file organization were not the only facets of modernization on display at the National Fire Insurance Company's new headquarters, though. As the nineteenth century gave way to the twentieth, the presence of female employees became an increasingly common feature of office life, and this resulted in new spatial arrangements and layouts. For instance, what is chiefly noticeable in the photograph of the Company headquarters' main hall is a sea of wooden desks. No people are included in the photograph, yet a description informs us that these desks would have been used by secretaries and stenographers—by women, in other words—while up above, on the mezzanine, space was reserved for the Company's individual agents, who would have been men. The space that these female employees would have occupied is marked by accessibility and vulnerability; anyone can enter into it, and the woman who labors within such a space therefore cannot help but appear constantly on display. By contrast, the mezzanine offices existing one floor above would have been harder to access. They would have also granted a birds-eye view of the work going on down below, among the ranks of female stenographers and secretaries.

The 1890s spike in female office employees occurred under the banner of the "New Woman." Sarah Grand had coined the term in an 1894 *North American Review* article, using it to advocate for a somewhat restrained, genteel approach to the issue of women's rights and independence. Grand declared that it was the New Woman's responsibility to "set the human household in order, to see to it that all is clean and sweet and comfortable for the men who are fit to help us to make home in it."[13] These declarations, though couched in domestic terms, extended to the public sphere and, in particular, to the office that, as an ascendant middle-class workspace, aspired to the same standards of taste and gentility as the middle-class home. As the historian Carole Srole additionally explains, stenography and clerical work provided socially acceptable outlets for middle-class women's nascent career ambitions to the extent that the female stenographer became emblematic of the New Woman movement. "The stenographic establishment, its media and schools . . . privileged this representation of stenographers as New Women by refashioning them as independent and ambitious that is, just like men."[14] If their ambition was to appear "just like men," though, the physical space of the office provided a continuous set of reminders that these female employees were, indeed, anything but.

Having been ridiculed for years because of its reputation for wastefulness, the office started to take itself more seriously toward the end of the nineteenth century, as it anticipated shifts toward a more full-fledged version of modernity in the twentieth. With that increased seriousness came the performance of gendered hierarchies and divisions. Women who were employed to work in offices were made to appear vulnerable and accessible to all. As receptionists, they were expected to be accommodating and friendly and to do their feminine damnedest to make the customer feel at home, allowing their own ambitions to appear subordinate to those of male senior employees. As the character Pam, one of the more famous exemplars of the female office receptionist, puts it in the original pilot episode of TV's *The Office*, which first aired in 1995, "I don't think it's many little girl's dream to be a receptionist."[15] Female office employees were brought into the fold, at first, to answer to male supervisors and to perform menial tasks like dictation and copying—the kind of work that Melville's Bartleby, years before, had starved himself in order to avoid doing. As middle-class male office workers became a more expected part of the social landscape and of the economy, female office workers appeared on the scene to do the jobs that men no longer "preferred" to do. And they did them in public, under the constant scrutiny of male bosses and supervisors who derived secret and, sometimes, not-so-secret pleasure from the act of watching them.

By the 1920s, the social codes governing much of office life had calcified along with the furniture and the physical layouts. The writer Sinclair Lewis, for example, created an archetypal take on all this routinized perving in the form of *Babbitt* (1922). Lewis's protagonist in this novel, George F. Babbitt, works in real estate and his office contains all the usual trappings: tile floors, neutral tints, "chairs of varnished pale oak," "desks and filing-cabinets of steel painted in olive-drab"—even a "new watercooler!" His office also contains a pool of female secretaries and stenographers, chief among which is the "rather pretty" Miss Theresa McGoun. Babbitt's position in the company commands respect and, thus, relative privacy; his own office is described as a "coop with semipartition of oak and frosted glass" (a cubicle, that is). Meanwhile, Miss McGoun performs her work from a desk that is placed in the middle of the office's central floor. This positioning enables Babbitt's lascivious surveillance of her. He fantasizes about an affair with Miss McGoun, which does not come to fruition, and eventually acts out his desires for rebellion through one with a female client. In both instances, the motivation is the same: Babbitt views sexual misadventure as an antidote to the anesthetizing realities of office life.[16]

In Babbitt's office of the 1920s, we observe how notions of panoptic "openness"—introduced decades earlier, along with female employees—formed the basis of the modernized, twentieth-century office. This spirit of openness stood in direct opposition to nineteenth-century taste that, when put to use within the domestic sphere, favored cloister-like nooks, narrow corridors, and intimate spaces. Privacy, in the modern age, was a privilege, not a right; it had to be achieved and earned through hard work and was therefore viewed as a goal that announced an individual's attainment of a certain level of success. In the meantime, low-ranking office workers and flunkeys were compelled to labor in communal spaces that simultaneously allowed for the surveillance of their work. All of this was in keeping with a host of new insights that had been developed by Frederick Winslow Taylor who, back in the late 1800s, had begun work on his theories of scientific management, which argued in favor of using empirical methods to increase labor productivity. In particular, Taylor's theory of "soldiering" posited that the idea of a work ethic was, to a certain extent, contagious. Taylor, writing in 1911, declared soldiering to be "the greatest evil" plaguing the contemporary workplace. He believed that modern workspaces might be designed so as to discourage soldiering and to, instead, encourage productive behaviors via a similar, but more strictly managed, system of peer pressure. That system hinged on making work *visible*—both to those who were overseeing it and to those who were doing it.[17]

If industriousness was contagious, then office workers, once corralled inside of a communal space that was also within sight of a boss or manager, would be induced to work harder together. But productivity is really only the beginning of the story where open floor plan offices are concerned. As Hunnicutt points out, labor leaders and union activists were campaigning in the early decades of the twentieth century for shorter working hours and, in the 1920s and 1930s, politicians and business leaders started to come around to the idea that *leisure* itself could, in fact, be productive.[18] This meant allowing for certain levels of leisure within the workplace, something that the open-office plan paradoxically also made more possible. The consummately accessible and penetrable core of an open-office space meant that workers could also access each other in order to socialize, share resources, compare notes, and collaborate.

New Office Aesthetics

The open space of the office thus transitioned from being one built for control and, in some instances, quasi-sexual surveillance, to one built for ease and accessibility. And as white-collar clerical work became the norm for larger proportions of the twentieth-century workforce, the open floor of the office became more of a coeducational space, too. As a construct, though, it proved resistant to innovation; for decades, few significant changes were introduced to plans that had been developed in the 1890s, which meant that the vast majority of open-office spaces wound up looking more or less like the central floor of the National Fire Insurance Company's headquarters in Hartford, with its sea of wooden desks arranged in uniform rows and all facing in the same direction, and with its tall arched windows permitting that desired "flood" of natural light. This practical, basic design did not receive an update until the 1930s, when Herbert F. Johnson Jr., president of SC Johnson and Son, Inc. (known at the time as Johnson Wax), hired the renowned architect Frank Lloyd Wright to design the company's new headquarters, which were to be located in Racine, Wisconsin.[19] Wright's "Great Workroom" would come to be regarded as an epitomic achievement that helped to launch the mid-century heyday of the American office.

At the time, Wright's portfolio consisted mostly of designs for private homes, along with a few public works. A single corporate project, the Larkin Administration

Building in Buffalo, New York, formed the only exception. The Larkin Building (1906) was gorgeous, short-lived, and, unfortunately, destined to meet with a wrecking ball only decades later in 1950. It improved upon the more morose office designs of the 1890s in featuring a light and airy central chamber that benefited from overhead skylights (see Figure 2).[20] Aesthetic flourishes, meanwhile, sought to disrupt the rigid verticality of the building's interior, with carved columnar supports, free-standing sculptures, and custom light fixtures announcing a holistic sense of artistry and attention to detail. The sociologist and aesthete Lewis Mumford proclaimed the Larkin Building "magnificent . . . like some enigmatic temple in the midst of a black industrial desert—contradicting but not suppressing the ugliness and disorder around it."[21] In his designs for the Larkin Building, Wright did not aim to radically revise the panoptic qualities of the traditional office layout, with its centralized "steno pool" positioned in plain sight, on the ground floor. But he did tinker with it in subtle ways, opting for verticality over a more conventional horizontal orientation and flanking the central atrium space with a series of stacked balconies. There was a problem with this scheme, though: Wright's architectural style was marked by the flow of natural light, but the stacked balcony design meant that certain levels of the Larkin Building were relegated to the shadows. It was a design that he would more or less abandon and reverse in his plans for the Great Workroom at Johnson Wax, where construction began in 1936.

FIGURE 2 Artist David Romero's rendering of the interior of the Larkin Administration Building in Buffalo, NY. This was the first of only two office projects designed by the architect Frank Lloyd Wright and was demolished in 1950. Image courtesy of David Romero, Hookedonthepast.com.

The idea was to create a vast and monolithic interior space that would give the impression of a vast and monolithic *ex*terior space—namely, a forest. Rather than a space apart, Wright envisioned an office that might bring the world of white-collar work into greater harmony with nature and repair some of that history of separation between the two. In a famous interview with Mike Wallace, Wright was asked whether or not the immensity of nature and natural forms made him feel small. "On the contrary," he answered, "I feel large, I feel enlarged and encouraged, intensified, more powerful."[22] It was these feelings of power and mastery that appeared on display at the SC Johnson headquarters.

As with the Larkin Building, Wright's plan for the Great Workroom centered on the harnessing of natural light. He wanted to create "an exhilarating environment" for the Johnson employees and natural light, as he saw it, held the keys to exhilaration and to worker productivity, as well.[23] There was a problem, though: Wright's trademark linear aesthetic involved a flat ceiling projected over a wide open floor, and this meant that vertical structures would have to be used to support the roof. It also meant that the roof itself couldn't be made wholly out of glass, which had been his original idea. In order to solve this problem, Wright opted for Pyrex glass tubing instead of glass sheets and used it in both the ceiling and in the outer walls of the building. The tubing allowed for greater stability and had the added benefit of refracting and bending the light. This reduced glare and lent a natural-seeming glow to the space, functioning much like a clerestory does in a cathedral.

Elsewhere in the Great Workroom, Wright put the logic and vocabulary of nature to work. He devised lily pad–like columns to support the ceiling's immense network of glass tubing, calling the design for the columns "dendriform" (literally, "tree-shaped"). These were fashioned from concrete that had been reinforced with steel and mesh and attached to the ceiling by way of hollow, ringed bands that he similarly dubbed "calyxes."[24] The whole design sought to elevate the space of the office by placing it on par with gothic cathedrals and the wonders of the natural world. In Wright's vision, organic spaciousness met with linear rigidity in a way that argued for, and then boldly celebrated, modern man's dominance over nature.

Meanwhile, Wright developed whole suites of office furniture—including desks, chairs, and mailboxes—that were meant to reinforce these twin aesthetic schemes. The desks, like the building itself, eschewed strict right angles in favor of rounded corners, and they mimicked the building's overall structure in being similarly composed of three distinct levels. The sparse design also discouraged clutter, with built-in filing cabinets and swinging drawers that granted access to files while encouraging tidiness and organization on the part of the worker. These accoutrements, like the carpet and the walls of the Great Workroom, were done in Wright's signature color, "Cherokee Red" (Hex #79413a).[25] It was the same hue—a blend of maroon and brown that had supposedly been inspired by the rich, red earth found in Oklahoma, previously known as Indian Territory—that he employed throughout his other architectural projects, including the Fallingwater residence in Pennsylvania. The Cherokee Red furnishings give an impression of soil, out of which the dendriform columns with their petal-like calyxes appear to grow wild.

Wright's work at the SC Johnson headquarters marked the beginning of a new era that saw the office transition from being a simple, spatial necessity to an emblem of intellectual and creative life. But it's important to note that Wright's designs did not consciously seek to alter the overall layout of the modern office, or to challenge existing connections between that layout and those previously mentioned practices of surveillance. Wright wanted to build a beautiful office, and his visions for that beauty amounted to a kind of brandishing of aesthetics. The splendor of the Great Workroom was meant to "exhilarate" workers' senses while also cajoling them into docility. Indeed, so central was the question of aesthetics that, for Wright, it trumped everything else, including practical necessity. Employee bathrooms, for instance, were installed well out of site beneath the Great Workroom and were accessible only via steep sets of descending spiral stairs. This made going to the bathroom quite a chore for the first generations of workers who populated the Great Workroom—almost all of whom, at first, were women. Photographs from the 1930s and 1940s reveal that the Great Workroom, for all of its aesthetic innovations, relied on a familiar organizational scheme with the secretary pool positioned at stationary desks on the main floor, beneath the watchful gaze of male administrators whose offices were, once again, to be found on the mezzanine above.[26]

The most remarkable part about the material history of the office, then, might well be its persistence. From its beginnings in medieval scriptoria, to its nineteenth-century development, to its aesthetic zenith in the mid-twentieth century, the office has remained a largely consistent and, thus, formally legible space. This is why offices are so instantly recognizable to us, regardless of function or purpose or design. Offices are sites of creative activity and innovation yet, as objects, they defy much of the innovation they purport to produce. The twentieth century itself reads as one long, protracted, tug-of-war between a very limited range of options for office design.

As the case with Wright has shown, the office has long been viewed as an aesthetic playground, but that manipulation of surface details conceals a kind of organizational stability that stretches back centuries. The particulars might change, but the form of the office remains resilient. Indeed, that resiliency is what modern companies like WeWork now seek to exploit. By establishing their so-called coworking sites nationwide and providing mobile office memberships to their customers, these companies are cashing in on two core truths about offices: the first is that white-collar workers still want them, even when it's possible to do their work elsewhere; and the second truth is that an office is an office is an office, and the structural components that define them amount to little more than walls designating *a space apart*. It doesn't matter what happens within that space. What matters is that the office exists to contain and consecrate whatever *might* happen.

2 THE OFFICE AS STOCKPILE

Indestructible Things

Though it is born from space, an office comes to life in its objects. Our relationships with office spaces are bracketed by all the many *things*, large and small, that they contain. This occurs as an extension of the role that the office has played throughout history, which involves the stockpiling and allocation of resources, as we saw previously in Chapter 1. Objects like desks and chairs, specialized machinery, and materials like paper and ink are central to the operations of the office and, at least throughout the twentieth century, office work would have been unthinkable without them. But these things comprise a small portion of that overall stockpile. There are still the potted plants and paperweights to be reckoned with, the desk ornaments and rolodexes, the trashcan basketball hoops and automatic return golf putters. These objects also belong to the space of the office, even if their functionality is less clear or less imperative than, say, that of a pencil or a computer.

Take, for instance, the humble filing cabinet, an object that, perhaps more than any other, has synecdochally stood for offices and office life. What the filing cabinet does, in practical terms, has to do with the organization and containment of paper; it separates and stores paper away so that it may be easily located again. But in larger, more metaphorical terms, the filing cabinet enshrines ideas about efficiency and bureaucratic management. It contains and protects; it separates and delineates; it grants, or else prohibits, access; it is easily navigable; and it is solid as a rock, able to withstand catastrophes like flood and fire. It is, in other words, a symbol of the well-managed corporation and of the office that such a corporation would aspire to call home. The offices of today have fewer filing cabinets than they once did, but the logic of "files" and "folders" hasn't gone anywhere: this, after all, is how we still talk about the items stored in digital hard drives and on our cloud-based accounts.

Filing cabinets have assumed an outsized role in office environments since the early decades of the twentieth century, when they were first marketed for use.[1] We meet a particularly remarkable one in Tess Slesinger's 1934 novel *The Unpossessed*. Professor Bruno Leonard, having toyed with the idea of starting a literary magazine for almost a decade, is enraged when a filing cabinet gets installed in his campus office because its arrival signals the conversion of his fantasies into hard, material realities. He judges this object to be "profoundly disturbing by its concrete presence" and anxiously wonders, "Where there's a Filing Cabinet . . . can the Magazine be far behind?"[2] For Bruno, the filing cabinet feels like too much of a commitment, materially speaking, because it has to be paid for, and that means that his magazine, which doesn't yet exist, has to start turning a profit. The pressure of seeing his dreams evaluated in such a vulgar (but also highly realistic) fashion incites him to panic.

> . . . Immediately he saw himself as assistant editor of a Filing Cabinet; he saw the whole thing complete, in its concrete form; complete with office desks and typewriters, lavatories, water-coolers, telephones on hinges, office girls named Miss Diamond, waste baskets, desk calendars, erasers tied to drawer knobs, fire extinguishers, supply closet, bench in the reception room, wire baskets for incoming mail, wire baskets for outgoing mail, all ticketed, docketed, billeted, and in all four corners threatening the editorial desk.[3]

Bruno views the filing cabinet's arrival not just as the start of an intellectual or business venture—the magazine, that is—but as the launching point for a whole course of material accumulation.

The objects that lend shape to the everyday world of the office double as receptacles for workers' anxieties—about their success or output, about their social status, and about their individual worth. This is due, in part, to the way that many objects have been historically introduced and folded into the space of the office for the sake of *replacing* human labor. The long history of swapping humans for machines within office settings has resulted in a situation where objects and equipment are often viewed as being, at the least, on par with and, at the most, as *superior to* their human operators, as we saw with the *Busy Office, Busy People* example in the Introduction. As such, objects appear as indispensable to the history and life of the office as the humans who populate it.

Objectifying the Office

Though the earliest versions were made from wood, steel filing cabinets—along with other types of steel office furnishings—debuted in the early 1900s as a popular means of keeping paper records safe from fire. This, combined with its growing use in the construction of skyscrapers, led to a kind of fetishization of steel as *the* material undergirding modern, civilized culture. As the architectural historian Alexandra Lange explains, "As buildings grew taller than fire truck ladders could reach, the market grew for all-steel office furniture, replacing heavy, flammable wooden cabinets."[4] Whereas wood, the material of the nineteenth century, had given rise to cozy, enclosed, private offices, steel formed the basis of new aesthetic demands aimed at openness and accessibility.

Thanks to steel, large, open floorplans became possible for the first time, "unobstructed by columns and unobstruct*ing* to the free flow of files," according to the media theorist Shannon Mattern.[5] And this meant more room for *stuff*, including filing cabinets but also new types of equipment and machinery, which were introduced in order to make the human machine of the office run more smoothly. Much of that new equipment was also made from steel, a fact that helped to reassert the material's aesthetic dominance over the space of the office. In a 1949 secretarial handbook, for instance, female secretaries are encouraged to make sure that they appear tidy and "well-groomed" so as to match the steel equipment in the office. This idea is bluntly conveyed via the statement, "Typewriters are streamlined; secretaries must be too."[6]

But with open floorplans came new challenges relating to efficiency and movement. As the office management specialist, John William Schulze, argues in his 1913 book *The American Office*, "eliminating movement about the office as much as possible will do much toward increasing the output of an office."[7] In order to do that, Schulze recommends dividing up the open space of the office logically in order to "determine the route of an order through the office."[8] More efficient routing means less time wasted on the part of employees and less money wasted on the part of the company. How does one go about dividing up an open space without sacrificing all of the original benefits associated with its openness, though? The answer, according to experts like Schulze, is through free-standing partition walls, better known as cubicles.

Today, many regard the cubicle—that most maligned of all office architectural clichés—as a recent invention. Nikil Saval, for instance, emphasizes how 1960s open-office plans more or less mandated the modern, carpet-covered version that we all know and hate.[9] But a wealth of historical evidence shows that they had, in fact, been in use for decades before the so-called Action Offices of the '60s took over. Frank Wheeler in Richard Yates's *Revolutionary Road*, for example, gazes upon an "aisle of cubicles"[10] in his workplace in 1961, years before the Action Office's 1968 debut.[11] And Schulze, for his own part, was advocating in favor of these "part partitions," as he calls them (albeit somewhat redundantly) as early as 1913. He had a good reason for doing so, too: noise.

New office machines dating from the end of the nineteenth century—including the telephone (1876), the mimeograph (1886), and the ever-evolving typewriter (which enjoyed wide use beginning in the 1880s)—had made the office a very noisy place. The playwright Sophie Treadwell, for instance, casts the sounds of office machinery as a ceaseless sonic backdrop in her 1931 work *Machinal*, which is about a young female clerical worker who goes insane and murders her husband.[12] Add to this mechanized melee the use of materials that refract sound rather than absorb it (like steel, glass, and concrete), and it's easy to see how acoustic control over the space of the office became a pressing, modern issue. "Part partitions," or mobile dividers, helped to minimize noise and, at the same time, became an important first step on the road toward objectifying the modern office. They transformed individual workstations into self-contained units and helped solitary workers to internalize their status as micro-components or "cogs," as they are so often called, within the larger machine. There was little room left over for human subjectivity in this setup since, as Schulze observes, in a well-regimented and controlled office environment, "it becomes second nature for [an employee] to place all of his thought upon his work."[13] Idiosyncrasy was viewed as the enemy of efficiency and output, and employees were encouraged to act and look as little like the humans they were and as much like the objects that surrounded them as possible.

In the same way that steel created durable office furnishings and "streamlined" aesthetics, screening for candidates' appearance and "health" was supposed to lead to the establishment of a more durable and streamlined workforce. That process included asking questions of potential employees that most today would consider a violation of privacy, if not downright illegal. Schulze, for example, provides an interview template in his *American Office* that includes questions like "Are you a member of any athletic, social, or church organization? What are they?" and "Do you engage regularly in athletic sports? What are they?"[14] Physical examinations, performed by a company-approved physician, were also a regular part of the hiring process and used to assess an employee's "fitness" for work.

The pointedly discriminatory nature of these procedures was supposed to help the employer make a sound investment in their labor force. But it also served as a way of warding against idiosyncrasy and making homogeneity the mantra of the modern office.

Injecting "Flair" into the Office

As the office grew and its contents became more uniform in appearance, objects became important for helping employees to maintain a grip on their own humanity. At first, they might have been limited to potted plants or framed photos—unheard of in the more rigid offices of the early twentieth century but becoming more common by the 1960s. For instance, in a 1963 newsreel produced by the Rank Organisation in England, female office workers' desks at the Shell Centre in London sport ferns and drawings done by their children. Though they work in an open floorplan office, on the walls nearby some of them have even taped up magazine clippings or pictures of nature scenes.[15]

Such privileges, of course, had been previously enjoyed by higher-ranking executives for decades—it's easier to get away with personalizing a private office than a workstation located on the main floor, because for personalization, you really do need walls. But the office had been in existence for centuries before the idea of "personalization" through office décor and objects was permitted to grow among its lower ranks. Beginning in the 1960s, office design manuals began to crop up, focusing on the creation of planned aesthetic environments within the office. In most cases, these efforts started with executives' private spaces and then bled outward to include common areas, cubicle clusters, and individual departments. That growth did not occur so much in opposition to concerns for "efficiency" and "sanitation" voiced by Schulze and others a few generations earlier but, rather, in response to a new reality: "white-collar" office workers, to use Upton Sinclair's and, later, C. Wright Mills's preferred title for them,[16] were now, for the first time, outnumbering blue-collar industrial workers.[17] The work of the mind had eclipsed the work of the body, at least in many industrialized and industrializing nations, and those legions of working minds needed to be stimulated and encouraged via nourishing, aesthetic environments. This conversion led, on the one hand, to successive attempts to market the Action Office designs created by Robert Probst—designs which would lead, in the end, to yet more uniformity. At the same time, though, it also led to the mandated introduction of flair into the office environment.

"Flair" is the word used by the character Joanna's boss in the iconic film *Office Space* with reference to the quirky buttons she is required to wear as part of her waitress uniform. But, as a concept, it also finds itself at home in the modern office. The film presents an analogy between service work and office work in less-than-subtle terms, as both Joanna (played by Jennifer Aniston) and Peter (played by Ron Livingston) seek to escape from the drudgery of their respective jobs. Flair is what is supposed to make the job, whatever it is (and whatever it is, it clearly sucks), look palatable and okay so that guilt doesn't have to enter into the transaction between employee and customer. But though it is supposed to provide a means for self-expression, flair actually has very little to do with the *self* of the worker. "You do want to want to express yourself, don't you?" Joanna's boss (played by the film's director, Mike Judge) asks her,[18] intimating the fact that, far from constituting a personal choice, flair is actually a professional obligation.

Flair translates to architecture on the corporate level and to *objects* at the level of the individual. An Instagram search of the hashtag #deskflair, for instance, yields thousands of pictures of displays that include everything from dolls, to miniature Christmas trees, to ironic signage ("Define *urgent*"), to elaborate succulent arrangements. The whole array, in fact, serves as a testament to both the breadth of the term's usage and *Office Space*'s success in adding it to our lexicon. But it also highlights a set of fascinating complications: flair, as you might recall from that scene in *Office Space*, presents something of a double bind in that it is both a tacit requirement and, supposedly, a method of self-expression. But is this the way it is understood by these legions of Instagram users? Are they, like Jennifer Anniston's character, questioning their right to refuse or resist flair, even as they collect likes on the pictures they post to the Internet? Or, after having been mandated for decades, has flair lost its compulsive sheen and turned into something real and sincere?

In order to get at the heart of these questions, it's useful to think about the history of flair and such seemingly nonessential objects in the workplace. That history ostensibly starts with the genre of objects known as "executive toys." This genre itself is so well-established that one can find linguistic counterparts in both French (*gadgets de bureau*) and German (*managerspielzeug*). In each case, the word or phrase in question refers to a suite of objects designed with two primary purposes in mind, according to the journalist Julie Lasky: (1) "sit[ting] in a workplace or home office" and (2) "[being] fiddled with."[19] Executive toys, as the name implies in plain English, are meant for those in the upper echelons of the corporate ladder—those, in other words, whose status affords both time and leisure. In contrast to the worker who is stationed down on "the floor" and not expected to have much of either, the boss is allowed and even *expected* to indulge in creative laziness. As such, I think Lasky sells executive toys somewhat short when she describes them as only having the twin functions of display and play. What an executive toy *means* is time. This is its third but also its primary function—to direct attention to an executive's status within the company and the freedom that comes with it, to flatter and consecrate his access to unstructured time.

Time and creativity, according to a very old formula, are the core ingredients of innovation. It's a formula that the writer Gertrude Stein, even, helped to advance via the statement that

"It takes a lot of time to be a genius. You have to sit around so much, doing nothing, really doing nothing,"[20] and it is one that continues to exert an influence on the logic surrounding the expenditure of time within the white-collar workplace. If one is permitted more time in their daily routine, according to this formula, it is because their time is more valuable in the first place, and because they are, as well. The same goes for space, since executives, according to the environmental psychologist Ronald Goodrich, are "like rock stars." Whereas "people at the bottom of the hierarchy are task oriented," those at the top require extra space and more elaborate settings in order to carry out their work as "idea generators, deal makers, socializers."[21] More than simply serving as distractions, then, executive toys have been used to lend concrete shape to the immaterial act of thinking and to announce one's right to the extra time and space that is required for imagination.

Take, for example, all the "toys" that have been created in support of what is likely the oldest executive pastime: smoking. Ashtrays are, arguably, the original desk ornament. When C. C. Baxter in *The Apartment* (1960), played by Jack Lemmon, gets his first promotion to a private office, it comes with a rather basic-looking ashtray. The ashtrays get fancier as you go up the chain, though, as Baxter's boss, Mr. Sheldrake, has no fewer than three in his office, including a free-standing floor ashtray. And in the film version of *The Big Clock* (1948), the answers to an office-wide mystery are eventually located inside a carved, decorative cigarette box that sits on the boss's desk.

Among the more memorable examples of office smoking accoutrements is Don Draper's roulette wheel cigarette holder from the show *Mad Men*. Variations on the spherical design were common in mid-century offices, sometimes featuring a globe instead of a roulette wheel. When one lifts the lid on the top of the sphere, a fan-shaped array of cigarettes falls forward. In *Mad Men* and other shows or films like it, cigarettes are primarily used as a device for the suspension of conversation or action. They buy time, in other words, as the acts of extracting a cigarette from a decorative holder, lighting, inhaling, tapping the ash and then placing it in an ashtray affords the speaker several seconds of contemplation. Don Draper and his colleagues frequently use them to this effect in the show; in fact, the very first time we meet Draper, played by Jon Hamm, in the opening scene of the show, he is smoking while jotting notes for a Lucky Strike cigarette advertising campaign.

Smoking is essential to the work of the office executives at Sterling Cooper because it lends physical or gestural reality to the act of thinking—an act which might otherwise appear as so much wasted time (and film). But even more than that, the history surrounding the use of smoking accessories in executives' offices demonstrates the difficulties that those at the top have had of "looking busy," and the wide range of objects that have been designed to help them do that. A cigarette affords a pause, yes, but not an inert one. There is, after all, action taking place; the cigarette smoker is inhaling nicotine in order to fuel his creative energies and keep them running at top speed. This compares to the way that office machines might require fueling or maintenance in order to continue running efficiently. As such, while they might appear somewhat gratuitous, desk ornaments like ashtrays and executive toys—to a similar extent as machines like computers—are actually doing important work on behalf *of* the office.

In many cases, the ideas and principles behind certain popular executive toys were developed in the nineteenth century (or earlier) but were not successfully marketed until much later, in the twentieth. This is the case with the Newton's Cradle (also known as the "Executive Ball Clicker"), which grew out of seventeenth-century experiments involving pendulums. These experiments sought to demonstrate kinetic energy even before Isaac Newton, for whom the toy is named, came along and presented his theories regarding the laws of motion. The Newton's Cradle didn't appear on office desks, though, until the 1960s, after it was given its name by the English actor Simon Prebble and then first sold in Harrods department stores beginning in 1967. This history renders the device's appearance in the Coen Brothers film *The Hudsucker Proxy* (1994) as something of an anachronism. In it, a Newton's Cradle sits on the desk of the character played by Paul Newman, even though the action takes place in 1958, almost a decade before it would have been available for sale. Throughout the film, the swinging of the pendent balls on the Newton's Cradle marks the passage of time, which is an important theme in the film. During one critical scene they even appear frozen in midair as time comes to a standstill for the characters. This is indicative of the film's somewhat lax and stylish approach to representing historical realities, in light of which complaints about anachronism are probably pretty superfluous anyway.

These kinds of executive toys look, on the surface, to be pretty silly. They don't really do anything except buy or mark time for those who possess them. But as Simon Prebble, the man behind the first commercially viable version of the Newton's Cradle once explained in response to being asked about its function, "What's it for? . . . If you have to ask, it's not for you."[22] Executive toys are not only "hired," in a sense, to lend life and personality to the office but to erect subtle barriers between the people who work there. In *Mad Men*, Don Draper interrupts the scene with a toy drinking bird—another classic example of this genre that debuted in the 1950s—by reminding his employees that they have work to do. His admonishments stand in contrast to the vast majority of scenes that take place within his own private office, where he does little more than smoke, drink, and nap. In addition to serving as flair, then, it's clear that executive toys function as markers of privilege. They denote superiority and its all of its attendant entitlements.

But does the continuing popularity of this genre of objects, as I have called it, spell more time on the part of the average office worker? Have the workdays of secretaries and accountants come to resemble those of the big brass at the top, with extra time left over for leisure and play? Of course not. In fact, office workers are probably working more than they ever have before. The Bureau of Labor Statistics, for instance, puts it at an of average forty-four hours per week for Americans—a 7.8 percent rise over what would have been the average four decades ago, in 1979.[23] And because, after having logged all those hours, white-collar workers are less likely to take home any tangible products in connection with that work, it stands to reason that office paraphernalia would assume a large and increasingly momentous role in their working lives. Toys and signage, pens and stationery, staplers and paper clips, inspirational posters, obsolete machinery—these things form the material residue of a life lived amid the stockpile of the office. An attempt to exert control over one's surroundings is an attempt to inject meaning into the anonymous space of the office. It doesn't matter if those attempts include decorative displays of Pez dispensers (as with some of my own former colleagues), a life-sized punching bag of Bozo the Clown (another former colleague), or a homemade lamp in the shape of Darth Vader's masked head (yet another). What these attempts collectively amount to is an insistence on idiosyncrasy—on a fight for differentiation between subject and object.

Perhaps it is this desire to represent the human side of work that explains why, from a cultural standpoint, we are so drawn to texts that show us scenes of someone quitting their job at an office. The process of packing up—of seeing one's belongings distilled into a few banker's boxes worth of stuff—sticks with us in these scenes because it brings home the small, material realities of the big, amorphous office experience. There is, for instance, the scene in the 1999 film *American Beauty* where Lester, played by Kevin Spacey, sails through the office with a single banker's box hoisted high upon his shoulder and a look of elation on his face. That same year gave us the movie *Fight Club* and another memorable quitting scene, wherein Jack, played by Edward Norton, stages a fight with his supervisor. He emerges from it victorious and bloodied, pushing a shopping cart filled with office supplies—a "telephone, computer, [and] fax machine" to accompany the "fifty-two weekly paychecks"[24] and air travel vouchers that he has settled for in lieu of pressing assault charges against his boss. And in *Office Space*, which *also* premiered in 1999 (making that year something of a banner one for stories about offices), a disgruntled employee, Milton, burns down the office and symbolically "quits"— ostensibly over a fight involving a stapler. In these scenes, triumph wears the guise of a reallocation of objects and resources. The stuff that once legitimized one's occupation of the space of the office gets hauled away and reinserted into a hoard of personal effects that, collectively, conveys an idea about how the worker "adds up" to something, both inside and outside of the context of their work.

It is this concern for "adding up" that animates some collectors' desires to accumulate office antiques. In the last section of this chapter, I'll turn to the discussion of obsolete objects and the people who love them. Items that passed through corporate environments with great rapidity and were designed, in many cases, with obsolescence specifically in mind get to live on through their collections. Most of the items in them haven't been necessary or useful for a very long time, but that doesn't mean that they have stopped *meaning*, or stopped speaking on behalf of their owner's impressions of the office.

Beautiful Machines

Thomas A. Russo started the Museum of Business History and Technology after retiring from a long career as a dealer of office machines. He had begun collecting equipment decades earlier through his involvement with the Business Technology Association, which had installed its own museum at its headquarters in Kansas City in the 1980s. But when that venture folded, Russo relocated much of the equipment to Wilmington, Delaware, establishing a new museum in the building that had once housed the offices of his company, Delaware Business Equipment. Operating on an appointment-only basis, the museum has received high praise from the likes of *Atlas Obscura*, a website that serves as a guide for peculiar, off-the-beaten-path travel destinations. Among the museum's contents are hundreds of nineteenth-century typewriters, cash registers, and adding machines, and an original Xerox 914 copying machine, which debuted in 1959 and is displayed alongside a vintage advertisement featuring our old friend, Brother Dominic.

Some of the machines work; some of them don't. But functionality is rather beside the point for Russo, who explains in a 2016 film interview, "There needed to be someplace where you could go and actually see these machines on display." He recalls, for instance, touring the office equipment archives at the Smithsonian and seeing "beautiful machines . . . stacked on top of each other. It was just terrible." His own museum, by contrast, was created out of a desire to see them all treated with respect. In the interview, Russo speaks with tenderness about the various objects in his collection, but falters when it comes to diagnosing his own motivations as a collector. "I do want the children to remember us,"[25] he says at one point, gesturing to the hundreds of machines that surround him in a way that makes the "us" all the more confusing. Who is "us"? The white-collar workers of yore? And how are those people tied to these machines—all of them lovingly arranged in glass display cases with catalog tags dangling—that looms in the background? How might we better remember the offices and office workers of yesterday *through* such objects, and why ought we to try?

I had hoped to find out some of the answers to these questions by paying a visit to Russo's Museum of Business History and Technology. But when I called to make an appointment, a rather sad-sounding voice informed me that it had closed. This was in spite of the fact that a news article dating from only six months earlier had mentioned the museum and suggested that it was still in operation. I tried to squeeze in a hurried inquiry about the machines—if the museum was closed, what had happened to them? The sad-voiced speaker, though, was vague: "Oh, they're still around." It was a response that brought home the obvious but nonetheless essential difference between object and subject, between machine and man. One sticks around; the other doesn't.

Indeed, anxieties about mortality often lie at the heart of a collector's hoard, regardless of the theme or nature of its contents. Where office equipment is concerned, such anxieties doubly reflect the apprehensive character of office work that, as we have seen, is often governed by threats of obsolescence. An office worker who reflects upon on a multi-decade career can't help but be confronted with the memories of tools and machines that have come and gone and, with them, specialized skills and knowledge and *time*, as well. The impulse to freeze time—to restore dignity not just to the machines themselves but to the workers who wrangled with and then, eventually, mastered them—is a palpable component of these collections. And there are many of them.

In researching this book, I corresponded and spoke directly with a number of people who continue to collect office equipment. Some of these collections, like Russo's, are private and run out of the collector's home; others, meanwhile, have been formally folded into larger, existing museum collections. Such is the case with Dietz Typewriter Collection, which is housed at the Milwaukee Public Museum and grew out of the personal collection of Carl P. Dietz, who donated of 113 machines to the museum back in the 1930s.

Dietz was active in Milwaukee politics and proud of his adopted hometown, having relocated there with his German immigrant parents in 1881. He was especially proud of the role that Milwaukee played in the history of what was, in the 1930s, one of the most important machines on the planet. The typewriter, as Dietz saw it, had helped to put Milwaukee on the map and it deserved formal recognition.[26]

I spent some time at the Milwaukee Public Museum inspecting items from the Dietz Collection, among them a charming and bizarre 1853 prototype called the Jones Mechanical Typographer (see Figure 3). With this rather cumbersome forerunner to the modern typewriter, the user doesn't so much *type* as manually position a rod on a wheel that is marked to indicate the positions of individual letters. The whole thing resembles a miniature version of a printing press, even more than a typewriter, but it was among the first designs to incorporate the idea of a rotating platen. That's the part of the typewriter around which the paper is secured and wound, and it would prove to be essential to later, more advanced versions of the machine. The Dietz Collection possesses the only remaining specimen of this particular patent model that for all its bizarreness paved the way for the ones we know and recognize now, and for what was nothing less than a revolution in the world of the office.

Using the Jones Mechanical Typographer would have required much more work than handwriting, or even printmaking, which helps to explain why it wasn't commercially successful. But it started engineers down

FIGURE 3 The Jones Mechanical Typographer, an 1853 forerunner to the modern typewriter. Dietz Typewriter Collection, Milwaukee Public Museum, Catalog Number E47377a-b, Accession Number 13890. (Author's photo, used with permission from the Milwaukee Public Museum.)

the path toward the QWERTY keyboard (which was also invented in Milwaukee and debuted as part of the first commercially successful model developed by Scholes and Glidden, who later sold their patent to Remington). The residue of all that labor was still upon it, too: I noticed that, attached to the platen, there was a scrap of paper with typescript, holding the same position that it had held for more than 150 years. Some person typed it—arduously, and with great care since early typewriters like this one employed striking action that worked from the bottom up, thus hiding the lines of fresh type from the person who was typing (and making typos all the more likely). I gently rotated the platen to get a peek at the rest of the typescript, which turned out to be a transcribed version of the poem "Hohenlinden" by Thomas Campbell. *On, ye brave / Who rush to glory . . .*

For those who collect them, there is much romance to be found in these old machines, even if there was originally little to be found in the work that they performed. It is the deepening chasm between the two—between the mundanity of offices and office work, on the one hand, and the emotionally charged mementos that we are left with, on the other—that gives rise to that romance. It is a desire to look back on years of immaterial labor and, after all is said and done, hold something in your hand at long last.

3 THE OFFICE AS HIERARCHY

So it's goodbye to the sunshine
goodbye to the dew
goodbye to the flowers
and goodbye to you
I'm off to the subway
I must not be late
I'm going to work in tall buildings.

JOHN HARTFORD, "In Tall Buildings" (1976)

Inventing the Corporate Ladder

Though an office can be located almost anywhere—in a strip mall, a coffee shop, a suburban office park, or even in one's own home—it is perhaps at its most quintessential when found inside a skyscraper. This is because skyscrapers stand as obvious symbols of hierarchy, and hierarchization is sacred to the meanings and functions of the office. These buildings protrude from, and then come to define, a city's skyline through displays of what the French philosopher Henri Lefebvre calls "arrogant verticality."[1] They epitomize not only power but, likewise, the so-called corporate ladder that is supposed to be the path to its attainment.

Skyscrapers and the offices they contain lend solid shape to fantasies of upward mobility and ascendancy. But we also know them to be vulnerable. The collapse of the World Trade Center's twin tower office facilities following the attacks of September 11, 2001 brought all that vulnerability and fragility to the fore for American audiences, but it was there all along. Since its beginnings in the early decades of the twentieth century, American culture has been drawn to the idea of the skyscraper, narrativizing its innerworkings in an effort to reckon with those latent feelings of vulnerability. And central to that vulnerability is the fear of falling—both literally and figuratively—from the heights of distinction to the level of mere paeons on the street or, worse, somewhere even further below.

In his 1961 novel *Revolutionary Road*, Richard Yates has his protagonist, Frank Wheeler, muse upon the prospect of such descendance. As a child, Frank marvels at the Knox Building in New York City—hardly a skyscraper at only ten floors, but still the tallest building he's ever seen up close and, significantly, the location of his own father's office. "Up and up and up the tiers of the windows rose, each smaller and more foreshortened than the one beneath, until their ever-narrowing sills and lintels seemed to merge. Imagine falling from the very top floor!"[2] Frank's ruminations are furthermore brought to life in the Coen Brothers' 1994 film *The Hudsucker Proxy*, which opens with the suicide of Waring Hudsucker, CEO of the fictional Hudsucker Industries. A routine board meeting taking place on the highest floor of a New York City skyscraper is interrupted by Hudsucker, who rises from his seat, breaks into a run, and hurls himself through the window. It takes him exactly thirty seconds to fall from the forty-fifth floor to the street below and to become, in the words of Paul Newman's character, Sydney Mussberger, "abstract art on Madison Avenue." His precipitous descent stands in contrast to the decades that it took him to build his company up "with his bare hands," as another character observes.[3] The overall idea is that hierarchical rise is a slow and onerous business, while falling tends to be fast, catastrophic and, often, extremely messy.

Waring Hudsucker's suicide in the opening scenes of *The Hudsucker Proxy* mirrors one described by the author Kenneth Fearing almost fifty years earlier. Fearing's *The Big Clock* (1946) is a noir-style thriller that has been adapted for the screen three times. It's chief narrator, George Stroud, works for a media conglomerate called Janoth Enterprises at their corporate headquarters in Manhattan. The company, as he explains, "fill[s] the top nine floors" of a building that also bears its name, with the various floors housing the offices of various Janoth publications. Stroud works for the magazine *Crimeways*, located on the twenty-sixth floor, and reflects that

Down the hall, in Sydney's office, there was a window out of which an almost forgotten associate editor had long ago jumped. I occasionally wondered whether he had done so after some conference such as this. Just picked up his notes and walked down the corridor to his own room, opened the window, and then stepped out.[4]

Stroud's musings in this scene foreshadow the fate of his boss, Earl Janoth. The book ends with a newspaper headline: "EARL JANOTH, OUSTED PUBLISHER, PLUNGES TO DEATH."[5] That these events more or less match the one in the Coen Brothers' film *The Hudsucker Proxy* (with a character named Sydney featuring in both) suggests a kind of cultural lineage. But such coincidences also help to cast the skyscraper as modern-day Thanatos. No one who is prone to standing and gazing out the window from an upper floor of a skyscraper is safe from thoughts of *What if?*, these texts remind us.

Our collective fears of falling are exacerbated by the hierarchized modern office. In her classic text on the subject from 1989, Barbara Ehrenreich diagnoses the mindset of what she calls the "professional middle class" (PMC), also known as yuppies, in order to find out how this group of people became less sympathetic toward those beneath them. By way of an answer, Ehrenreich analyzes yuppies' feelings of vulnerability; unlike with the wealthy elite, whose assets may translate to hard currency, "capital" for the PMC comes primarily from "knowledge and skill . . ." and "these cannot be hoarded against hard times, preserved beyond the lifetime of the individual, or, of course, bequeathed." Because of its reliance on softer, more ephemeral forms of capital, the PMC lives in perpetual fear of falling and descending from the positions that its members fought so hard to win in the first place. This fear steels yuppies against the prospect of generosity or welfare for the poor and instills a miserly outlook, according to Ehrenreich.

Ascendance, as films like *The Hudsucker Proxy* make clear, is supposed to be hard-won and slow, while descendance can happen in a matter of seconds—literally, as in the case of Waring Hudsucker. But even as it dramatizes and literalizes Ehrenreich's arguments about "falling," the film also offers a cautionary tale about what it means to rise in the first place. Following Hudsucker's dramatic suicide, the board, led by the guileless Sydney Mussberger, embarks on a scheme to deplete the company's stock in order to prevent Hudsucker's shares from being released for purchase by the public. Their decision to replace him with "some jerk"[6] off the street sets the stage for Norville Barnes's rise to the office of the president and, subsequently, his physical rise from the mailroom—located below ground at Hudsucker Industries—to the forty-fifth floor.

In this way, the film offers an introductory lesson in dramatic irony: *we* know that Barnes's rise is superficial, not based on merit, and thus fated for implosion. But *he* doesn't. While this disconnect makes for comedy and hijinks in the short run, it reinforces a set of principles regarding the sanctity of the hierarchized office. The climb to the top isn't supposed to be easy, the film reminds us, and it isn't supposed to be fair. If it looks like it is, on either account, something's amiss—and comeuppance can't be too far behind. Norville Barnes, who is played by Tim Robbins, ends up physically falling from the forty-fifth floor, just like his predecessor. He is saved, though, by Hudsucker himself, who appears in the form of a benevolent angel in a scene that recalls Frank Capra's *It's a Wonderful Life*. The outcome is not the point, though, so as much as the threat of falling itself, which looms large in this film much as it does elsewhere in the modern imagination.

The Rise of the High-Rise

The skyscraper literalizes the fear of falling and inscribes it upon the consciousness of the American office worker. It does this in no small part through its designation as the nation's chief "vernacular" architectural form, as the geographer David Harvey sees it.[7] It translates the American reliance on hierarchization—and white-collar workers' fears of losing their grips on particular rungs of the corporate ladder—into space that one can experience, inhabit, and walk around in. It gives physical shape to ideas of impermanence and vulnerability, which makes people afraid, and *that*, so the theory goes, makes them better workers.

For instance, Keith Payne, a neuroscientist, describes how offices, along with modern workplaces, are invariably "organized as hierarchies." As a space, the office excludes and consecrates; it denotes something different and separate, as we saw in Chapter One. Along the way, though, it performs the equally important work of sifting and ordering its contents—especially its *human* contents. This is why, according to Payne, workplaces like the office often serve as the primary arena for peoples' engagements with hierarchization and its (generally negative) consequences. "The workplace is where most people experience inequality most directly on a daily basis," Payne argues.[8] Whereas Americans' faith in equalizing schemes like democracy normally throws a veil over inequality and hierarchization, offices operate in blatant deference to them. Hierarchy is not just a practical tool to be used within the office setting; it's the whole point. Everyone wants a spot at the top, but the pyramidal structure of office relations—which mimic labor relations playing out on a broader scale elsewhere in the economy—means that the vast majority are fated to duke it out down at the bottom. As Larry Ross, an ex-CEO and interview subject in Studs Terkel's wonderful 1972 book *Working* puts it,

> Fear is always prevalent in the corporate structure. Even if you're a top man, even if you're hard, even if you do your job . . . The fear is there. You can smell it. You can see it on their faces. I'm not so sure you couldn't see it on my face many, many times during my climb up.[9]

The form of the skyscraper not only makes these fears symbolically evident; it exalts and raises them to the level of gospel.

The development of the skyscraper form in the late 1800s and early 1900s was made possible by two inventions: the elevator and stronger steel. Prior to this era, proximity to the earth was actually viewed as an advantage. Most nineteenth-century offices or places of business were located on the ground floor, regardless of the height of the building that housed them. Upper floors, meanwhile, were deprioritized and reserved for other uses (including residential space, storage, etc.). The birth of the skyscraper, though, had the effect of reorienting Americans' priorities; it made distance *from* the ground (and, by extension, proximity *to* the open vista of the sky) suddenly and somewhat paradoxically desirable. Much of that desirability stemmed from notions of exclusivity. Offices located on ground floors lend an impression of accessibility and openness. This is why pools of female laborers, employed as secretaries or stenographers, would often be stationed there while their higher-ranking male colleagues would have their offices upstairs on the mezzanine, as we saw previously with Frank Lloyd Wright's "Great Workroom" at Johnson Wax. With the skyscraper, though, select office workers were able to insist on increasing amounts of distance between themselves and the "common" thoroughfares of the street, thus heightening the impressions of exclusivity and prestige associated with their labor.

They couldn't do it without elevators, though, which were introduced to ferry them to the upper floors of a building without making them work for it. The architect Rem Koolhaas, for instance, explains how elevators assign prestige by removing these select employees from the realms of the street and placing them on par with natural elements like air and light. He views the elevator as "the ultimate self-fulfilling prophecy: the further it goes up, the more undesirable the circumstances it leaves behind."[10] Higher floors thus become equated with higher status and upward mobility starts to feel like a mandate, rather than a goal. This makes the top of the skyscraper, in both real and metaphorical terms, a rather scary place since the only available routes leading from it point *downward*.

For instance, in the "Sandwich Day" episode from Season 2 of the NBC show *30 Rock*, Jack Donaghy, played by Alec Baldwin, gets demoted after making a play for CEO. His office is subsequently relocated from the fifty-fifth floor of 30 Rockefeller Center (which was completed in 1933, during the NYC skyscraper boom, and has a total of sixty-six floors) to the twelfth. When the elevator deposits him there, he discovers an austere, bureaucratic backwater. It is the functional inverse of his former digs up on the fifty-fifth floor, which included majestic views, sumptuous leather furniture, a fully stocked private bar, and an overly accommodating personal assistant. By contrast, on floor twelve, Jack is greeted by an ancient mailroom employee, a slovenly man with a false mustache, and a one-eyed receptionist. Directional signs point to the physical plant, a storage room for Internet servers and, cryptically, an "elephant graveyard." A handwritten sign, meanwhile, informs him that "No Nut Food" is permitted. Everything appears to be broken, from the neon lights that spasm and strobe overhead, to the signage ("Floor 12" is missing both of its o's), to the elevator itself, which wheezes shut, barring Jack's escape. It's the same elevator that he took down from the fifty-fifth floor, of course, but on twelve, it falls instantly under a spell of gross incompetence. Jack senses that either he or his career—if not both—will meet its end here, amid this ignominious hellscape of ruin and ineptitude.[11]

In addition to the practical functions described above, though, the elevator also allowed for repeatability within the form of the skyscraper. Whole buildings could be designed around a central nerve system made from elevator shafts, with each additional floor laid out identically to the one below it. This resulted in both efficient construction and aesthetic uniformity throughout the building, but it also made things cheaper because it meant that very big buildings could be built upon relatively small or compact pieces of urban land. Over time, though, it also had the effect of reinforcing feelings of sameness and uniformity on the part of the office workers who used these buildings, as Koolhaas lamentingly observes. With repeatability as their mantra, skyscrapers furnish "evidence of . . . sheer territorial multiplication"[12]— or, to put it in slightly different terms, *colonization*. When the bluegrass music icon John Hartford sings about "going to work in tall buildings" in 1976, he does so not with elation but, rather, with a sense of gloom.[13] For Hartford, the "tall buildings" in question are all the same; they sequester the office worker and bar their access to natural elements like sunlight and air, and they are all filled with the same kinds of people. Koolhaas notes that all of the repeatability is strategic, too, since workers who look and act like each other can easily be replaced *by* each other, if and when necessary.

This brings us back to Yates's *Revolutionary Road*, where much of the conflict hinges on anxieties about similitude, replaceability, and characters' doubts about their overall purposes in life. At first, Frank Wheeler believes that he is distinct from the "endless desperate swarms" of white-collar workers who appear alongside him every morning, flooding the streets and stations of midtown Manhattan before being "swallow[ed] up and contain[ed]" by the nondescript edifices of the office buildings located there. Inwardly, he mocks these "tiny pink men in white shirts, forever shifting papers and frowning into telephones, acting out their passionate little dumb show under the supreme indifference of the rolling spring clouds."[14] Frank's blind reliance on color descriptors like "pink" and "white" furthermore points to the racialized history of both skyscrapers and the people who occupy them—people who Frank sees as being one and the same. Such racialized assumptions are common, scholar Adrienne Brown points out, even if the reality is much more complex. According to Brown, in much of the culture of the early twentieth century, "skyscrapers are depicted as changing what it meant to both see and be seen as a racial subject."[15] Frank's assuming that everyone who goes in and out of a skyscraper is white like him is indicative of this bias, but also of widespread fears about homogenization.

The tragedy in *Revolutionary Road* comes when Frank is no longer able to keep up the lie regarding *his* own exemption from the crowd. Throughout the novel, we see him struggle and fail to do that, growing more desperate with each repeated attempt. One of those attempts involves a steamy but short-lived extramarital affair with a secretary, lending credence to one of the oldest and most beloved clichés of office life: the office affair.

Step into My Office, Baby

Within the office place, affairs become a hallmark means of brokering the frustrations experienced by workers like Frank. We saw this previously with Sinclair Lewis's Babbitt: a dawning awareness of homogeneity and replaceability leads to a desire to lash out and distinguish oneself by any means possible. What's significant, though, is how the very concept of the office affair crosses over and mediates between different positions within the workplace hierarchy. Bosses sleep with their underlings—classically, their secretaries—and middle managers like Frank in *Revolutionary Road* follow suit, emulating the practices of those at the top in what amounts to so much trickle-down philandry.

For instance, in *Mad Men*, Peggy Olson's arc gets its jumpstart thanks to an interoffice affair with the character Pete. This affair is all we know about her for the majority of the first season, even as she begins to haltingly ascend the ranks at Sterling Cooper, landing a promotion to the position of copywriter in the final episode of that same season. Peggy's new job serves to physically remove her from the female-only, openly accessible "floor" of the office and from its pool of infinitely available secretaries and receptionists. Observing as much, Joan acerbically tells her, "Remember, just because you now have a door, don't forget that once you didn't."[16] The door in question—even though it leads to a cramped, windowless, shared office space—is everything, for Joan as much as it is for Peggy. It means, as Virginia Woolf outlines in her *A Room of One's Own*, intellectual freedom and the right to self-absorption, qualities which, though they are brought to fruition within the abstract realms of the mind, "depend[] upon material things."[17] It also signals relative privacy, which is a privilege and thus something that has to be fought for and won.

Peggy eventually gets a *real* room of her own, but it takes her the length of an entire season—another thirteen episodes—to do so. After she gets it, Pete, her former lover, inquires point blank about her tactics, asking "How did you swing this?" She responds with the lie that she has intuited is the rest of the office's version of the truth: she tells Pete that she's been sleeping with Don Draper, her boss.[18] It's untrue, but it makes far more sense than the story of her meritorious rise. In essence, her lie corroborates Woolf's point about how "when a subject is highly controversial—and any question about sex is that—one cannot hope to tell the truth."[19]

We have been imbibing the story of the office affair for so long, it has become a regular part of our cultural and social diet. Lewis's Babbitt's affair in 1922 looks much like Fearing's George Stroud, who sleeps with his boss's mistress in *The Big Clock*, published in 1926; Nathanael West picks up the thread in his 1933 work *Miss Lonelyhearts*; Willy Loman cheats on his wife with a character known only as The Woman in Arthur Miller's *The Death of a Salesman*, from 1949; Frank Wheeler pursues an office "fling" with Maureen Gruber in Yates's 1961 novel; and on and on it goes. By the time *Mad Men*, a show about the 1960s heyday of the American office, debuted in 2007, it wasn't adding to that lineage so much as eulogizing it from the vantage point of a nostalgic present.

That is not to say that office affairs were on the wane by the early 2000s. Rather, it was the physical site that played host to the office itself—that was perceived to be dying. "Remember how much fun the office used to be?" was the question that *Mad Men*, and other shows like it, posed to its viewers. Remember the drinking, the carousing, the *affairs*? In taking a whole set of office affairs—Pete and Peggy (his coworker), Roger and Joan (his subordinate), Don and Rachel (his client)—as its starting place, *Mad Men* reinforces the supremacy of this narrative and the physical space that gave rise to it, mounting a claim for the intrinsic quality of both in the context of post-war culture. The office, the show argues, is part of our collective heritage, and so is everything that happens inside it.

But *how* does the office affair happen? What special machinery exists within the framework of the office to nurture and bring it about? To start, there is space: the higher up one ranks, the more private and more secure their personal space within the office is going to be. CEOs and bosses operate with expectations of on-demand privacy; the prestige associated with their positions compels trust and everyone assumes that, whatever they're doing, it's appropriate, necessary, and beneficial to the company. The second factor is time. The sense of trust that governs office leaders' claims to privacy is reflective of the trust that is likewise instilled in them through the system known as salaried labor. A boss's time is his own, so long as he meets the targets and goals that have been set for him in his contract. This is not the case for the wage laborer, who has to account for every single hour that she spends, or else fails to spend, working. *Her* whereabouts matter at all times to the company, since they are being compensated in piecemeal fashion and with deference to "the clock." In this way, a salaried employee is viewed as an investment; their value has already been decided upon, ahead of time, and rendered in contractual terms. In order to gratify their own decision-making, the firm places trust in these employees and grants them relative freedom with reference to both space and time, ingredients that are necessary to any extramarital affair.

In addition to these considerations, though, there is the aforementioned issue of fear. Office affairs, for those who figure lower down in the hierarchy, are viewed as one means of gaining advantage—either over a particular person (a superior, or one's immediate competitors), or else by leveraging one's limited power within the hierarchical structure. This is where the cliché of "sleeping one's way to the top" enters into the picture; sex can be used as a tool for emotional manipulation, so this thinking goes, even though emotions aren't supposed to be part of the equation within the office setting. Female employees like *Mad Men*'s Peggy Olson, it is assumed, will resort to this tactic since they are more likely to rank below men and less likely to possess the talent that would allow them to ascend by other means. But this is where the cliché loses much of its steam: if sleeping one's way to the top is such a common feature of office life, then why aren't there more women *at* the top, controlling and running the offices (let alone the companies they serve)? The notion persists even in the face of well-advertised facts about the dearth of women in corporate leadership positions.

Fear is clearly a great motivator, then, but I would argue that the office affair owes a lot of its staying power and cultural prowess to the conceptual divisions between home and work. Increasingly over the course of the twentieth century, the cultural and social life of the office began to unfold at a distance from domestic realities. In America, the 1950s and 1960s saw cities emptied of much of their residential contents through the process known as "white flight," whereby middle-class families relocated to the suburbs in response to racial and ethnic integration. For many white-collar office workers, this led to a situation where "work" meant one place and "home" meant another, with a distance of perhaps dozens of miles stretching between the two. In novels like *The Big Clock* and *Revolutionary Road*, as well as in shows like *Mad Men*, that distance is often reinforced through the structure of the narrative itself. Fearing organizes his chapters alternatingly between George Stroud's work and home, never allowing the two locales (or the characters who frequent them) to coexist within the space of the page; in *Revolutionary Road*, Yates presents Frank and April Wheeler as functionally and spatially separate during the working week—in different states, even, with Frank in New York and April back home in in Connecticut. And in *Mad Men*, characters like Don and Pete maintain girlfriends in the city while their families are located elsewhere in the suburbs. Pete even convinces his wife (also located in Connecticut) to let him get an apartment in the city, ostensibly for work purposes.

The development of the office as a space *apart*—detached, unique, and subject to its own rules and codes—has made the office affair an integral part of its social legacy and mythos. Today, Americans commute longer distances and for greater amounts of time than ever before, suggesting that for many, the gap between home and office has only continued to grow. According to one study, the fastest growing subset of commuters includes those workers who spend more than forty-five minutes to an hour a day traveling between home and work, while the proportion of workers with limited commutes (less than ten minutes) continues to shrink.[20] The result is a widening of the space between home and office, solidifying the image of each as a world unto its own.

Such illusions of isolation beget adages like *what happens at work, stays at work*. What's more, as the economist Andrea Komlosy shows us, that polarity is central to our very understandings of work and its veritable opposite, the home and the family. "According to the bourgeois family ideology of separate domestic and gainful spheres," Komlosy explains, "no 'work' [is] to be performed within the family,"[21] or within the spaces that it occupies, except by those who are excluded from inclusion within the family. This is why the stay-at-home mother does not get compensated for her labor while the white-collar, office-dwelling father, does: not because there isn't work happening on both sides, but because only *some* of that work takes place within a space that has been specifically marked for labor and compensation.

If work has to happen in certain spaces, like an office, in order to be considered "work," than does that mean that everything that happens inside such spaces *is*, by definition, work? The idea of the office affair subjects this correlation to further scrutiny, as do other forms of social engagement, like meetings and office parties. In the final section of this chapter, I want to turn our attention to the latter, and for a couple of reasons. First, because office parties show the office at its most ribald and so often serve as the launching points for office affairs—in our cultural imagination, if not necessarily in reality. Next, because office parties furnish one of the few spaces or occasions for the intermixing of the different components of the corporate hierarchy, allowing underlings to come together in the presence of bosses and superiors. And lastly because, culturally speaking, we seem to be obsessed with them.

Unwinding and Unraveling at the Office Party

In my own, somewhat idiosyncratic experience with offices and office spaces, holiday parties figure prominently. For instance, during my cubicle-dwelling days as a graduate student at Carnegie Mellon, the annual department holiday party afforded one of the only regular opportunities for interacting with the "stars" of the office. Among them was the poet Terrance Hayes, a MacArthur recipient and National Book Award–winner whose poetry I had read but who I almost never got to see in person, despite the fact that we "worked" "together." Both words, in this case, merit quotation marks: the first because Hayes, though he was, like me, employed by the English Department at Carnegie Mellon, rarely taught courses there, and never to graduate students; the second because, though he and I performed similar types of labor within the department, I couldn't be sure of the extent to which we did so in league or "together." Were we colleagues? Hayes was a professor, but he had never been *my* professor, so our history was not defined by the dynamic between teacher and student. We performed similar kinds of labor by teaching English classes, but the difference in our ranks lent wildly different meanings to that work. We both wrote, too, but to varying degrees and purposes; his writing went on to be published and vetted by critics, while mine was submitted in exchange for credits on my transcript. We shared the same space, in a technical sense, so our work took place alongside each other's, but that space was spread among the vast reaches of a building called Baker Hall, with the result being that our paths rarely crossed.

If anything was going to grant me license to use the term "colleague" in reference to my relationship with Hayes, the holiday party was it. There we would meet in the hors d'oeuvres line, and I would stumble through a conversation in which I tried to make it clear that I knew who he was and had read his work, even if the reverse was obviously not the case. I did this every year, my courage annually kindled by free wine, only to watch our relationship lapse immediately afterward back into the way things had been before, with him not recognizing me in the hallway and me pretending not to care. That was the substance of our collegiality, with the holiday party providing an occasional spike that, while it never lasted, always gave me something to look forward to.

Office parties—and holiday-themed versions, in particular—enter into the general discourse surrounding the cultural history of offices in a similar way. Office-centered television shows, for example, like to use them to close out a season and bring closure to different storylines.

Similarly, in the 1957 film *Desk Set*, a number of romantic and comedic entanglements culminate during the scene of an office Christmas party. The film stars Katharine Hepburn as Bunny Watson, who oversees an all-female group of office workers employed as reference librarians at the fictional Federal Broadcasting Network. Their jobs and livelihoods are threatened when a so-called efficiency expert, armed with many a Taylorist credo, is hired to, first, calculate the speed and accuracy of the librarians' labor and, second, to see them replaced by a computer of his own design. Toward the end of the film, Watson and her team prepare for what they have come to believe will be their last office Christmas party, since they expect to be laid off after the holidays. There is champagne and there is tinsel and there are voluminous taffeta skirts (this is the fifties, after all). But amid these signs of revelry, there is also gloom. One character sullenly wonders, "What do you suppose it'll be like here next Christmas, when we're gone? Do you think [the computer] will throw a party?"[22] These melancholic feelings are cast aside, though, when the librarians' office party combines with the one taking place across the hall in the legal department. There is a piano, along with a watercooler filled with red wine, and dancing ensues. So does romance, for it is during the Christmas party that Watson and the efficiency expert, who is played by Spencer Tracey, begin to acknowledge their mutual feelings for each other.

The Christmas office party scene in *Desk Set* provides a more wholesome gloss on what starts to look like a long-standing tradition in American culture. Racier versions, meanwhile, can be found elsewhere, including in movies like *The Apartment* (1960), where the holiday party includes a striptease, and *Mad Men*. In season four of the latter, the firm stages an elaborate Christmas celebration in the hopes of impressing a client who is considering jumping ship. Though they had been planning something small, Roger Sterling demands that they change party's rating "from convalescent home to Roman orgy."[23] A conga line, preceded by plenty of booze, helps to set the tone, which starts off as mirthful but soon declines into tawdriness. Don Draper, recently divorced, winds up in bed with his much younger secretary; this proves to be both the start and end of their relationship, as she is seen preparing her resignation at the end of the episode. A strikingly similar set of events, meanwhile, inspires the lavish festivities in the movie *Office Christmas Party* (2016), which repeats the watercooler-filled-with-booze gag from *Desk Set* (also featured in *The Apartment*), suggesting that there is a reliable source of comedy to be found in the appropriation of everyday office accoutrements.

What all of these festive reenactments point to, though, is the extent to which office social relations—despite, or perhaps actually *owing to* their hierarchical nature—mirror family relations. If we take, for example, the idea that roughly one-third of the average lifespan is supposed to be spent at work, then we can make sense of how the office starts to feel like an alternative home, with its human counterparts resembling a "second family." Insofar as the monogamous, nuclear family represents, in the words of Friedrich Engels, "the cellular form of civilized society," so does the office, with its emphasis on hierarchical divisions of labor, come to resemble and, in certain cases, rival that "conjugal system."[24] This is why holidays are traditionally observed within the space of the office, in many cases in direct defiance of the obvious differences (racial, ethnic, religious) that might separate and distinguish its members; this is why office Christmas parties, in other words, are a thing, mirroring the kinds of celebrations that would otherwise take place within the family and inside the home.

In another, less common but still popular take on the office holiday party, we see office personnel acting supportively and posing as each other's families. This happens in a memorable episode from the first season of *The Mary Tyler Moore Show*, which was one of the first television sitcoms to explore the significance and meaning of office work to the women who had already been doing it for decades. In "Christmas and the Hard-Luck Kid II," which aired on December 19, 1970, Mary, who is single, is forced to work on both Christmas Eve and Christmas Day after she volunteers to sub for a colleague so he can spend time with his family. Mary tries her best to remain upbeat about the prospect, but becomes frightened and depressed when, nearing midnight on Christmas Eve, she believes herself to be the only person left in the building. Several of her coworkers come to her rescue, though, showing up to keep her company during the last thirty minutes of her shift. They willingly supply the family that Mary does not yet have but seems fated to one day attain, given her winsome personality and social prowess at the office. The episode ends with the group's decision to stage a party of their own as soon as her shift is over.[25]

On the surface, these parties appear to have the effect of collapsing the space between work and home. Here, after all, is to be found another kind of family, and another kind of family gathering. Except in establishing what feels like a viable and convincing alternative *to* domestic relations, the office actually reasserts itself, arguing in favor of its uniqueness and its irreplaceability. While they purport to offer a break from work, though, office parties are, in the end, another form *of* work. This is clear given the people who attend them, who wouldn't know each other apart from their work, and whose very relationships are therefore a product of the social interface that is the office. In *Office Christmas Party*, for instance, two female employees express their mutual relief about being able to socially engage with each other while not talking about work, only to immediately realize they have nothing to talk about that isn't work.

The ubiquity of these party scenes in popular culture stems from a perceived need to represent these spaces and settings without actually associating them with drudgery or, well, labor. Everyone works; everyone can relate to the culture of work; but no one wants to watch or read about people *at* work. Office parties provide a dependable means of narrativizing the more glamorous or lighthearted side of office culture and the hierarchical structures that govern it.

Fragile Hierarchies

While it might be taken for orthodoxy inside the office, the concept of hierarchy has, in recent years, revealed itself to be an increasingly fragile one. For all the fear that it projects and its reminders about *replaceability*, the notion of a hierarchy is itself dependent upon conditions of relative stability. In other words, the corporate ladder requires something firm at its base in order to extend upward. In the past, that something firm took the form of visions of permanence. Permanent, salaried employees—even if they did not make up the entirety, or even the majority of a company's ranks—were always supposed to figure into the overall equation. In his book *Temp*, though, Louis Hyman shows how the American workforce, including white-collar work and office staff, has become increasingly temporary over time, with part-time labor now threatening to take the place of even formerly secure, stable positions within the corporate framework.

As the so-called gig economy continues to spread and infect new corners of the contemporary labor market, one cannot help but wonder about the longevity of some of the office hierarchies described above. They also cannot help but recall that the office, as Hyman points out, played host to some of the earliest efforts to make permanent jobs into temporary ones. Services like Kelly Girl (later rebranded as Kelly Services) and Manpower have been supplying short-term, part-time workers for service in office settings since the early twentieth century. The story of these companies and of the growing part-time labor force is about as old as the IRS Form 1099-MISC, which is used to assess taxes owed on short-term or contract work, and which debuted just over a hundred years ago, in 1918. The idea of a temporary workforce has been with us for a century now, and within the space of the office, it has only continued to metastasize. Historically, women and ethnic minorities comprised the bulk of the temporary workforce, filling jobs as office "temps" (in the case of Kelly Girl), seasonal agricultural laborers, etc. This was why, for decades, nobody worried about the temporary and insecure nature of these jobs, and this is why people are starting to now. With the casualization of not just the white-collar workforce but the *white* white-collar workforce, the opportunities for exploitation appear to be growing.[26]

Halle Butler's novel *The New Me* (2019), for instance, presents a story that, for women, is very old, even while it purports to be part of something that is burgeoning and new. Millie is a thirty-something-year-old, white Chicagoan who, in spite of her middle-class background and education, struggles to secure stable work. The novel follows her through a stint at a high-end design firm, a job that has come with the promise of permanence but that, like all the others before it, proves to be only temporary. As a receptionist, Millie is starved for meaningful work and stimulation, and this means that she can't quite commit to the permanence that she is supposed to desire; she is unwilling to go to battle for her own, permanent boredom. "The shit-eating is meaningless to me," she reflects acerbically.[27] Her resulting poor performance on the job is a symptom of her feelings of inertia; as a modern-day Bartleby, she doesn't want this office or this work, and would rather see her body starve instead of her brain.

If the corporate ladder is based upon ideas of mobility, then the world of temporary labor is based on conditions of forced stagnation. In Millie's world, that stagnation involves "merging, submitting" and "moving forward while staying in the same place. Moving forward *by* staying in the same place."[28] Recall previously, for instance, how the poet Ralph Waldo Emerson expressed his fears about how offices and office work might establish standards of professional ease and "stability," thus leading to a less active and creative American workforce. Through its insistence on upward mobility, and by a fostering a near-constant atmosphere of competition, the office of the twentieth century managed to temper some of Emerson's fears. But with larger and larger swathes of its twenty-first-century staff relegated to "temporary" or contractual status, one wonders if the gospel of climbing the corporate ladder will continue to resonate, or if its clerics will even continue to preach it. Companies like Amazon, for instance, have developed a reputation not just for temporary labor but for refusing to promote from within their own ranks.[29] Perhaps this is why 75 percent of Americans now reportedly believe that it is harder for young people today to secure a middle-class lifestyle, which would grant them access *to* the office, than it was for the generation that came before them.[30] Such statistics make Emerson's fears of office lethargy appear almost quaint. Skyscrapers once forced us to reckon with our fears of falling, but you have to envision a way to the top before you can learn the fear of falling from it. When you're starting from the ground without hopes of advancement, as so many young workers are today, a sinkhole starts to look like a more fitting metaphor than the Empire State Building.

4 THE END OF THE OFFICE

Beyond the Offices of the Future

History is a dumping ground for the so-called offices of the future. The vast majority of them already reside in the past now, with the Action Offices of the 1960s and the utopian designs of the 1990s dot com era appearing quaintly retro by today's standards. Like other forms of consecrated space—including the home, the church, and the library—offices have been the subject of futurist scheming for almost as long as they have been around and recognizable to us. Architects like Frank Lloyd Wright laid the groundwork for some of that prophetic tinkering as early as 1903, more than a century ago, and since then the office has continued to function as a container for visions of what may come.

But much of that tinkering ends up looking, in hindsight, more *re*gressive than progressive. Today, we laugh at the thought of the cubicle's capacity for improving the landscape of the office, just as we do at the sunken living rooms of the 1970s. Yet in the vast majority of large offices today, one can still find cubicles—even at companies like Google, which once made headlines touting its role in ushering in the "future of the office."[1] As a form, the office isn't just regressive, it's manifestly cyclical. Its proven knack for routinely presenting the old as something new makes it a prime exemplar of the adage about history repeating itself. Even more than that, though, it makes it a testing ground for an incipient crisis, one that today's "no-collar" workers may not be sufficiently prepared to confront.

The term "no collar" is used by some to refer to the sector of work that fosters a hybrid environment between humans and machines but, critically, relies on a mix of labor supplied by both, including robots. The critic Andrew Ross helped to popularize the phrase in a work of the same name published in 2004, and in it he explains how "liberalization of the workplace had followed much the same path as the liberalization of the economy."[2] The result in both cases, according to Ross, is decentralization on a massive scale, with workers cast not as contract-bound employees but, rather, "free agents" left largely on their own and forced to take responsibility for themselves. The office of the future, for no-collar workers, is not a place to make a lifelong career. Instead, it is a temporary and infinitely swappable container—a space like any other, where one goes to perform not specialized work but to tend and oversee the work of specialized machines.

The specter of crisis that now casts a shadow over the contemporary office and inspires, every few years, new ideas about what it needs to be and how it needs to look, is a crisis born from anxieties about sustainability. Having taken a tour of history's garbage dump and seen the remnants of its prototypes for the future, we can't help but see our own offices as vulnerable or insecure. And with the dismantling of the corporate ladder—which, if it stifled and intimidated workers of the past, it at least gave them something to aspire to—come bigger, more existential crises and questions. Why *this* work? Why here? Why now? And why me?

The crisis that is coming *is* the end of the office as we know it, but it's not the end of the office. For those at the top, pulling the strings and trading slices of the ever-shrinking pie that is "the means of production," in Marxist terms, the office is on the verge of becoming more important than ever. As with their private homes, the office will grow and evolve for this elite group of people, becoming more elaborate since there will be fewer plebs around to mess it up. New offices will rise, unabashedly monumental in appearance and scale, to serve smaller and smaller populations of workers. I'm not saying that companies will get smaller, rather that the vast majority of the people who remain contractually connected to them will, like the Uber drivers of the world, be increasingly asked to carry on independently, to complete their work in piecemeal fashion, and to tote the their laptops from place to place—to *be* their own office, in other words. The twenty-first century's office of the future presents a diptych of inequality:

on the one side, an ostentatious playground of privilege and elitism; on the other side, a Starbucks.

The former species is nascent and also already with us. In fact, the terrain has been forming for a few decades now, with companies like Amazon leading the charge by designing offices that do not look like offices and, for large swathes of its employees, do not function as offices, either. From these examples, it would appear that the white-collar, creative economy in America has outgrown the use of the word "office." Yet it continues to rely on it, cramming all manner of modern spatial arrangements into the word as though it were an ill-fitting, designer shoe. These offices don't exist to facilitate actual work—even the work of creative thinking, which they purport to inspire—so much as to exert a company's right to take up space, regardless of how that space gets used or what it's for. These spaces are more billboard than laboratory. They make a big show of breaking rules and of appearing anarchic and wild on the surface, resisting the kind of legibility that is the result of decades' worth of repetition. But beneath all that wildness there is to be found an essential kernel of emptiness, space in its purest and rawest form; beneath all the grandeur and the fireworks, austerity.

The Office as Shrine

Like many Americans, I work in an office, and also like many Americans, mine includes strange, living creatures with Latin names. I never asked for these officemates and, most days, I forget they're even there. But on the rare days when they call attention to themselves—when drooping leaves announce the need for water, or yellow fronds start to collect on the carpet—I remember how they came to me in the first place. The *Dracaena drago*, or Dragon Tree, came from Beatrice, who left my school for one in Indiana; ditto the *Ficus elastica* in the corner. My *Sanseviera trifasciata*, or Snake Plant, was once Becky's, but she took a departmental chair position elsewhere. And my *Pelargonium citrosum*, or Citronella geranium, belonged to Heidi before she quit academia in order to concentrate full time on her writing.

These officemates of mine are an exotic bunch—the Dragon Tree is native to the Canary Islands, for instance, while geraniums are most commonly found in southern parts of the African continent—but they are also a common feature of modern office life. They thrive indoors under semi-stable conditions, much like the human office worker. Since the 1950s, the decade that saw the growth of white-collar jobs in America along with its spatial counterpart, the modern office, researchers have observed positive correlations between aesthetically pleasing office environments enhanced by indoor plant life and apparent rates of worker satisfaction and productivity.[3] The American biologist E. O. Wilson went so far as to argue in his 1984 work *Biophilia* that our attraction to plants is demonstrative of "an innate tendency" in humans.[4] Wilson borrowed the term "biophilia" from the German philosopher Eric Fromm, whose original concept emphasized "*liebe zum lebendigen*" (or "love for the living") and the natural capacity for "growth, whether in a person, a plant, an idea, or a social group."[5] By contrast, Wilson's "biophilia" tries to explain our specific love for plants and nonhuman forms of nature, diverting the focus away from their roles within natural systems and, at the same time, their relationships with each other. While Fromm viewed biophilia as a societal objective that could only be achieved given a set of human-engineered advancements (security, justice, and freedom), Wilson changed the conversation by making it about loving the natural world enough to preserve it.

It is Wilson's version of biophilia, not Fromm's, that is chiefly on display at The Spheres, the "hybrid conservatory office building" located at Amazon company headquarters in Seattle, which opened in 2018. Amazon cites Wilson directly in much of its display and advertising materials, which are available to the public, unlike the interior space of the building itself, which is not. While certain ranks of Amazon employees are permitted access to The Spheres during normal working hours, the public must be content with a basement-level lobby area dubbed Understory, which speaks enticingly of the building's innovative features to an audience that is not allowed to actually witness them firsthand (except on official tours, which are offered twice each month). I was lucky enough to gain entrance to The Spheres recently in the company of Ira Gerlich, a contractor who works with but not for Amazon and whose company, evolution Projects, oversees the in-house dining facilities there.

From the outside, The Spheres resemble a set of Buckminster Fuller–style geodesic domes. They huddle side by side at the feet of construction cranes, amid the skeletal outlines of tomorrow's skyscrapers. In recent years, Amazon's presence has transformed Seattle's South Lake Union neighborhood, giving rise to numerous building projects. Across the street from The Spheres, for instance, a WeLive high-rise is underway. When it opens, it will offer "flexible, furnished" apartments that are available on a temporary basis, just as it has done in cities like New York and Washington, DC, in an effort to meet the needs of tech-sector employees. Through The Spheres' humidity-stained, transparent walls, one glimpses billboards over at WeLive— an offshoot of the popular office space subscription company WeWork—speaking in slogans of *Do What You Love* and *Live Better Together*. The idea is to capitalize on the increasingly porous divide between work and the less productive facets of human existence (passion, enjoyment, social interaction) through dorm-room-style living arrangements located only steps away from places like Amazon.

Over at The Spheres, a similar spirit of porousness and fluidity reigns, along with a pronounced sense of confusion. When I started inquiring about visiting The Spheres, I was repeatedly told that it was "not an office." (I was conducting research relating to a book on office design and my interlocutors seemed concerned that my time at The Spheres would be wasted.) This is in spite of the fact that The Spheres repeatedly bills itself as an office, calling attention to its

FIGURE 4 The Spheres at Amazon HQ in Seattle, Washington.

hybrid status as a 24-hour-a-day "nature conservatory" and 12-hour-a-day "workspace." In one of the promotional videos on display at Understory, Dale Albeerda, Principal Architect at NBBJ Architects (who designed The Spheres) explains how the building was inspired by historical designs for nineteenth-century conservatories, and how that inspiration was brought to bear upon the idea of the traditional office. "The typical office building is about enclosing as much floor space as possible," Albeerda notes, which explains why they look like boxes; The Spheres, by contrast, "are about volume" and the utilization of multiple dimensions in office design.

The 4,000 enclosed square feet of "vertical vegetated surface" is designed to stoke Amazon employees' creative furnaces by giving them alternative space in which to work and think. As Ben Eiben, the lead horticulturalist at The Spheres, puts it in another promotional video, "You feel a little bit more creative if you're removing yourself from all of the human implements and you're just out in nature."[6]

What are The Spheres like, and what kind of work actually takes place inside them? This is what I hoped to discover on my visit, which started off with a rather detailed security screening. I, along with my chaperone, had to have our access credentials checked and our photo IDs processed before earning the right to don red "Guest" badges and proceed through the checkpoint. Once inside, there is nowhere to go but up, as a series of stairs flanked by burbling water features climbs to the first landing (the site of what was a "grab-and-go"-style café offering readymade sandwiches and other items, now closed). The atmosphere inside is steamy and vaguely tropical, with the daytime temperature ranging from 72 to 76 degrees and the humidity capped at 60 percent for the sake of plants and humans alike. When the human workers go home at night, the humidity climbs to 85 percent to mirror the diurnal cycles that the plants, which hail from a variety of mid-montane ecosystems, are used to. A living wall or "vivarium" starts with tropical fish installed within glass tanks at its base and extends upward for several thousands of feet, the entire surface covered with species of fern and red-bristled bromeliad. It is the centerpiece around which an interlocking system of elevated walkways, stairs, nooks, and landings appears to swirl.

On one of those landings is another café, General Porpoise, which serves coffee and gourmet snacks. It is part of a legion of offspring that have sprouted from a James Beard Award–winning local chef, Renee Erickson, and on the day that I visited, it was the center of activity inside the building. Mind you, that activity was of a humble kind: a few employees—less than a dozen—appeared clustered around its outskirts, bent over their computer screens, badges prominently displayed on their shoulders. Others could be occasionally found elsewhere throughout the building, including in an upper gallery area fitted with lounge-style lawn chairs where I saw one employee awkwardly reclining with a laptop balanced on their knee. There are dedicated meeting spaces designed to accommodate small groups, including a circular "crow's nest" structure that extends out into the air, and a number of what I will call "coworking cages," for lack of a better term and owing to their walls being made from metal supports and wire mesh.

But there weren't very many people using these spaces. For all its being chock-full of organic material and life, the mood at The Spheres felt rather down tempo and, well, a bit dead. Ira tried to shed some light on this situation, noting that we were visiting on a Friday, though it seemed nonetheless significant to me that one of the two cafes had already closed within a year of the building's opening. I got the impression that The Spheres might be plagued by a sense of confusion, resulting in low use—that, and the somewhat onerous security procedures necessary for access. While I saw plenty of plants and waterfalls and tropical fish, plus the occasional latté, I didn't see a lot of *work* happening, including the work of tending and maintaining the plants, which must be substantial in order for the space to function and look its best. And this, I began to suspect, might be the whole point.

In *The Architecture of Neoliberalism*, Douglas Spencer observes the trend toward what he calls "techno-environmental immersion," which the so-called new architecture of the 1990s began to reclaim in the service of managerial practice.[7] Doing so involved placing an emphasis "on the design of open, landscaped and connective spaces" that were, in fact, engineered for a kind of deception. The idea, according to Spencer, was to eradicate the notion of strife from the work experience and to get the worker to see herself as a component of a larger, "natural" order. This was architecture made to "kill critique," and on two fronts.[8] The first vector of attack involved stymying critiques of a building's underlying design scheme through a focus on multifunctionality, which made the overall "plan" itself appear opaque. The second was to make the work itself immune to critique: if the worker did not actively associate "strife" with the work they were doing, they would be less likely to voice complaint about their position, about their rights and benefits as a laborer, about the company they worked for, or about the larger systems that might be supporting it. Rendering labor invisible was sacred to this project, too, guided by the theory that if a worker can't tell whether or not they're working, they'll be inclined to work *more*. This gave rise to managerial strategies "premised on informality, collaboration, and mobility"[9]—strategies lifted from the countercultural movements of the 1960s.

Which is all to say: there is a reason why The Spheres resembles geodesic domes. The utopian-communitarian designs of the 1960s gave rise to the architecture of labs and technology research facilities of the 1970s, with both focused on aspirational values like collaboration, play, and a spirit of global consciousness. The offices of Xerox Palo Alto Research Center Incorporated, when they opened in California in 1970, featured plant-festooned rooftops and came furnished with beanbag chairs. This is a history that challenges some of Amazon's claims to "innovation" as far as The Spheres are concerned, but also one that positions the company within a larger narrative about technological progress and utopian design. As the journalist and critic Charles Mudede puts it, "Haussmann's Paris is with us today in Seattle."[10] And in light of such a history, one can't help but wonder if The Spheres, given the riotous effects of nature taking place both within and without, will age as poorly, in both political and material terms, as some of the projects that came before it.

Despite some material differences, though, my experience touring The Spheres brought to mind my own office. I spied a cousin of my *Blechnum gibbum* (Silver Lady Fern) amid the fourth floor "fernery," for instance. I inherited mine from a plant-rabid former colleague who, like so many others, is also gone now. My workplace has been ravaged by austerity in recent years, resulting in forced retirements and a lot of "pivoting" to careers in administration, which have cast a pall over our hallways and workspaces.

A similar kind of emptiness makes the green-filled spaces of The Spheres feel more like a branding move on Amazon's part than a facility to be used by actual workers. It announces its company's good intentions to the world by erecting a monument to absence—the absence of nature in modern life, the absence of social connection within white-collar work, even the absence of affordable housing in cities like Seattle thanks to companies like Amazon. But it doesn't begin to alleviate the suffering caused by those absences, just as my collection of cast-off plants doesn't alleviate my feelings for the colleagues I've lost and the social interactions that once helped to buoy my working hours; rather, the work being done at The Spheres is the work of preservation. The buildings, which resemble glass jars, preserve an image of Amazon's supposed benevolence as a company and an image of neoliberal capital as growth, as opposed to absence and austerity. In both cases, the emphasis on the vessel's construction is meant to distract from the hollowness lurking inside.

Meanwhile, reports of deplorable working conditions at Amazon's many fulfillment centers have become a regular feature of the news cycle, making it hard to see The Spheres as anything but an oversized swear jar brimming with watery intentions—as the inverse, that is, of the material conditions experienced by the *average*, as opposed to elite, Amazon worker. While the differences between the two are many, the most salient one has to do with the way these buildings gesture toward, or else block out and void, nature itself. Where The Spheres are built largely of glass and so permit access to light, inspiring seemingly natural conditions for sociability and human collaboration, Amazon fulfillment center employees report "there's no windows in the place, and you're not allowed to talk to people—there's no interactions allowed."[11] Inside The Spheres, all is tranquil, with sound deadened by the immensity of the space, save for when timed jets release plumes of mist into the temperate atmosphere; at the fulfillment centers, though, all is chaos, with the "general hum of the building ma[king] it too loud to speak normally."[12]

What all of this points to is a new and disconcerting investment in old labor hierarchies. The distance between Amazon's sprawling fulfillment centers and its lavish Spheres complex is not unlike the distance between factory and office described in Chapter 1 with regard to Gaskell's novel *North and South*, even though that novel was written in the 1850s. It is the distance between protected, supportive working conditions—increasingly the privileged domain of the elite—and everything and everyone else.

You Can't Sit with Us

Even before my visit to The Spheres, I was acquainted with the idea of the modern, elite office. My introduction—and the inspiration behind this book, in fact—came years ago, back in 2016, when I was visiting some friends in Chicago who work in the tech sector. One of them was going to be celebrating his birthday over the weekend and was planning a party at his house, so the group decided to swing by another friend's lavish company offices with the goal of picking up free flower arrangements.

That's right: flower arrangements. My friend works for a high-profile software company who, as he explained, was having difficulties luring its workers into the physical office, since their work doesn't actually require them to be there. For this reason, the company had invested in a number of amenities (ping-pong tables, showers, lounges complete with napping couches) and services (in-house bartenders and caterers, floral arrangers) aimed at transforming the workplace into a more desirable and happening location. The florist was contracted to drop fresh flowers on every employee's desk on Thursdays; but since no one (still) used the office very much, we might as well swipe them for the party, they wouldn't be missed.

It being a Friday and nearing happy hour, our trip to the office to collect the flower arrangements wound up including a visit to my friend's "club" down the street, which I soon came to see as an extension of his elite office facilities. The "club" in question turned out to be the Chicago branch of Soho House, an enterprise that started in London in 1995 and, according to the company's website, proffers "a home from home for people working in creative fields." A home from home? What does that even mean? It means, in essence, work-adjacent facilities that are made available to members for work-adjacent activities, like networking (that is to say, drinking and dining). Soho House is not an office, but it facilitates and supports the life *of* the office from alternative—and self-consciously luxurious—digs. The Soho House in Chicago, which is only one of several international locations, has multiple bars and restaurants, a gym, a spa, a movie theater, and a rooftop swimming pool. All this and more is available to the "creative souls"[13] who qualify for membership, and who pony up the several thousand dollars per year in membership fees.

None of this is exactly new, of course. Gentlemen's clubs, after which the Soho House franchise would appear to model itself, proliferated throughout Britain in the eighteenth and nineteenth centuries, and later spread to the United States. At first, these clubs catered only to very elite populations, and then became popular among the upper middle classes. In the United States, a branch of them grew associated with specific universities and served as places where alumni could meet to socialize, conduct business, and, ostensibly, extend their collegiate ties. A similar idea inspired the formation of athletic clubs, which operated in much the same way while placing an emphasis on athletic facilities. These various clubs did not pretend to be offices in the strict sense, but they were a far cry from the alternative—that is, the domestic realm. They gave shelter to business interactions and furnished a secure, comfortable environment for office-related activities, like reading or professional lunch dates. They also, critically, provided an elite gentleman with a place to go that was *not* home to the wife and kids.

Today, Soho House locations harness much of the nineteenth-century spirit of the elite clubs of yesteryear, even as they claim to do otherwise. In their membership materials, for instance, they proudly state that "Unlike other club concepts, which often focus on wealth and status, we aim to assemble communities of members that have something in common."[14] That "something in common" turns out to be "a creative soul"—whatever that means. The criteria for membership are actually quite ambiguous, though the founder, restaurateur Nick Jones, originally envisioned members as being comprised of "young people working in film and media." Over the years, that ambiguity has resulted in a fair amount of controversy; in 2010, one of the New York branches culled its roster, aiming to excise those who fit a more traditional, suit-and-tie, corporate model and get the club back to its "creative" roots. Following what had been deemed "the purge of the suits"—where members were expressly asked not to wear suits inside the club so as not to diminish the creative vibes—the branch, located in the hip Meatpacking District, shed 500 members from its ranks.[15] The move served to make explicit what many had already assumed—namely, that "creative" meant not just elite but a certain kind of elite.

In pondering the many contemporary meanings of the word "creative," I asked my friend if "creative" could mean someone like me, a writer and professor. Could I join the elite roster at Soho House? He wasn't sure. During our dinner, though, I watched him greet several people from across the room, all of them his colleagues in the tech industry, itself the larger force behind the elite office movement. I decided to put the question of my own membership to the test, though not via Soho House.

In recent years, a number of competing, members-only, office-adjacent establishments have sprung up throughout the US to save the more privileged kind of creative worker from the ignominy of a Starbucks and the horrors of spotty Wi-Fi. Indeed, foremost among the amenities that appear on offer at these clubs is a reliable, high-speed Internet connection. Even though today, routine office work—like sending email—can take place almost anywhere, these clubs promise to make you experience a special kind of somewhere en route to the act of logging on. It's not just email: it's email as performance art. But the centuries-old aroma of snobbery and prestige, which at Soho House comes across in the polished mahogany surfaces and dark velvet upholstery, sent me looking for something more inclusive and, well, less devoutly masculine.

I found its effective inverse in The Wing, a female-centered network of coworking spaces that, like Soho House, has quickly spread to cover cities nationwide—and also like Soho House, The Wing draws self-consciously off of nineteenth-century club culture. On its website, it touts the history of "the women's club movement"[16] and the "pioneering women who provided each other with encouraging community at a time when they needed it most." In turn, it seeks to provide a space where professional women can not only gather to send email but can "find everyone from [their] next business partner to an enthusiastic running buddy."[17] Where Soho House skews masculine, The Wing skews feminine, styling itself as a workspace (more than a club) designed and built especially for women. That includes "materials . . . selected to optimize female comfort" and even warmer thermostat settings. As an *Atlantic* article explains, the thermostat at the flagship New York location is kept "between 73 and 74 degrees, appreciably higher than New York's mandated temperature of at least 68, and flouting typical guy-bod preference." Many of these features are thanks to Alda Ly, the architect who oversaw the creation of that first outpost and lent a "feminist's eye" to its design (in this case, "feminist" seems to translate to *a lot of pastels*).

I stopped by The Wing's Chicago location to tour its facilities and to witness firsthand the special "materials," which turned out to be nearly identical to those used throughout the nearby Soho House (located two blocks away in the West Loop), except, yeah, more pink. The most notable difference between the two establishments, in fact, was the lighting; where Soho House favors dark, intimate, hunting lodge interiors, the entirety of The Wing's office spaces were filled with natural light from large, floor-to-ceiling windows. This, combined with the pastel color scheme and white tile flooring, gave the place a turn-of-the-century ice cream parlor kind of feel. The opulent bathroom facilities were also designed with old-fashioned charm in mind, with surround-style vanity lighting, deco-inspired wallpaper, and complementary cosmetics stations. All of this gave the impression of a very narrow sense of femininity or femaleness that rivaled Club Soho's seemingly narrow interpretations of the word "creative." Though The Wing repeatedly bills itself as "a diverse community open to all" on its website, which also features testimonials from the likes of Alexandria Ocasio-Cortez, I wondered how precisely that particular sense of femaleness might be enforced: What about trans women? Would they feel welcome in this space? Were their "needs" part of the design scheme, too? Would they even be allowed inside it?

I live in North Dakota, which as yet does not have its own branch of The Wing and probably never will. And, anyway, I have an office already. But I was interested in looking into the prospect of gaining membership to an elite office like The Wing, if only to figure out what doing so might take—so I applied. A new location was set to open at the end of summer 2019 in Seattle, my hometown, and still a city where I find myself a couple of times every year. Plus, I thought, if I took advantage of the franchise-wide membership that grants access to all locations, I might occasionally have reason to use one in another city, like Chicago. (All of this is beside the fact that I was never going to be able to afford the $2,700 annual fee and so had no real intention of acting on the membership offer, if I was to even receive one.)

The membership process itself proved to be replete with quirks designed to reinforce The Wing's stated mission and values. Among them was the part requiring the applicant to produce a mini essay about how their professional work contributes to the "advancement of women." I was still hunting for answers to my ongoing questions about the eligibility of trans women and nonbinary individuals, as there were none to be found in any of the promotional materials. In fact, the only mention of trans people I could find was on a page talking about scholarship initiatives that were awarded to members of the community. Yet the essay question plainly said *women*—no asterisks, no caveats. Hoping that more answers might be found in another section of the application, I banged out an essay about my work as a scholar of women's literature, my academic training in gender studies and queer theory, the courses I had taught on these and related subjects, my ongoing research, my service record, and so on. But the questions kept multiplying for me, especially after I learned that the New York City Human Rights Commission was investigating the organization for possible gender discrimination. In the beginning, men were not permitted inside any of The Wing office spaces, even as guests, a policy that was dropped only recently in January of 2019.[18] Those changes haven't yet been registered on The Wing's blog, though, which continues to operate under the name *No Man's Land*. And at the same time, I couldn't help but suspect that, as with Soho House, there might be secret criteria for membership that placed an emphasis on specific kinds of creativity—namely, the kind believed to exist exclusively in the tech and start-up worlds. (In explaining its Membership Benefits, The Wing explicitly describes a "thriving digital community.")

I didn't need this office, but I wanted to find out whether or not I was good enough to even pay for the privilege of setting foot inside it. I wanted to test the limits of my own elite inclusion, even as a business blog warned me that 8,000 women had previously joined the waiting list for the Brooklyn location alone.[19] The whole project was taking on a decidedly sorority-ish flavor, which only intensified as I read one writer's account of gaining admission to the DC location and then declining to join. From Mimi Montgomery's article in *Washingtonian* magazine, I learned that one of The Wing's founders was the real-life inspiration for one of the characters on the HBO series *Girls*, previously dated the fashion photographer Terry Richardson, and had had her wedding featured in *Vogue*.[20] I knew it then: this was not my milieu, and "creativity" was code not just for coolness, but actual stardom.

The Exclusionary Office

If it's the stars, not the grunts, who claim the offices of the future, what is the future of the office? For many of us, it's a scenario that might just make us long for the days of private cubicles and open floorplans. The early 2000s saw the rise of the "coffice"—

that is, the trend of treating public coffee shops as private offices—along with the growth of Wi-Fi. In 2003, 802.11g Wi-Fi became standard as the first robust frequency able to offer semi-reliable wireless Internet connections that could extend to cover public spaces. Suddenly coffee shops could be offices for those who needed them to be, and that population's numbers were growing. Why commute into the city when all you needed was a chair and an outlet at the local Caribou? Some coffee shops pushed back against the office-ication of their spaces. One I used to frequent in those days, Victrola Coffee on Seattle's Capitol Hill, refused to offer Wi-Fi even as late as 2007, with politely worded placards informing customers that this was a "conversation-focused" coffee shop and not a study hall. But the tide of connectivity could not be contained; more than a decade later, Victrola has multiple locations throughout the city, and they all have Wi-Fi, of course.

The turn toward coffices might already feel like a thing of the past, but it is very much a part of the future of office work. The futurologist Nicola Millard, for instance, predicted in 2014 that a majority of white-collar workers would make the shift to working remotely, whether from coffee shops or their dining room tables. "There is no reason why knowledge workers shouldn't all be working flexibly in five years' time."[21] Five years later, which just happens to coincide with the time of this writing, the flexible side of office work has surely grown, but it has also inspired a backlash in the forms of Soho House and The Wing. And the prime motivator behind that backlash, I would like to argue, has to do with control.

It stems from a desire to shelter elite, white-collar creative work—the sacred provenance of the office—from the perils of an anarchic working environment and, in particular, from the creeping stain of poverty.

In April of 2018, on the heels of the #BlackLivesMatter campaign that gripped the nation and brought long overdue attention to the injustices of American racial politics, two black men visiting a Starbucks in Philadelphia were arrested. They hadn't ordered drinks or purchased anything and, according to employees, were guilty of loitering and causing a nuisance. The news of their arrest prompted accusations of racial profiling and the franchise responded by closing its 8,000 locations for a day of "sensitivity training." Beyond that, though, it ushered in a new corporate policy stating that a Starbucks "guest" was not obligated to make a purchase in order to use the space, including the bathrooms. The goal was to avoid future instances of racial profiling, whether accidental or not. Starbucks later walked that policy back somewhat with the added clarification that sleeping and drug use would not be permitted inside stores.[22] But the damage had been done in the eyes of many, who were quick to voice their fears on social media about Starbucks becoming the nation's largest homeless shelter. As one Twitter user put it, "Goodbye @Starbucks. I'd say it was nice knowing you but I never really understood the attraction. Enjoy life as a soup kitchen."[23]

Starbucks, formerly the accessible American heart of the coffee trend, had fallen from grace in the eyes of many of its customers, who vowed to take their laptops elsewhere. Of course, elite establishments like Club Soho and The Wing were already on the rise years before the Philadelphia incident forced Starbucks' hand and forced them to convert informal practice into company-wide policy. The founders of these venues had discerned a growing market for elitism and privilege in office work that rose in tandem with the expansion of chains like Starbucks and also with a decreasing dependence on dedicated office environments. What happened in Philadelphia in 2018 only served to emphasize the issues associated with doing work in coffee shops—or existing in public at all—and, hence, the need for controlled, exclusive, but above all, *exclusionary* workspaces. The future of creativity itself, it seemed, was at stake. As with failure, there seems to be a fear of contagion where poverty is concerned, resulting in greater efforts toward quarantining.

But along with all of this white-collar white flight—because that is arguably what we're really talking about here—what the shift toward members-only offices additionally reveals are rampant anxieties about the dismantling of bureaucratic hierarchies; where a generation ago an employee would have dreamed of working their way up the corporate ladder in order to score a coveted corner office, now they can simply bypass the whole ladder business and buy themselves an exclusive seat in it. But—and this is crucial—that seat no longer comes with the status and privilege (or salary) that it once did; in fact, all of those perks have been taken off the table. You can have the beautiful office, if you're willing to pay for it on your own, but you can't get promoted in a manner that says you actually deserve it. You'll never be the boss, so you might as well settle for being the boss of yourself and renting that nice view for the time being.

If there is an office of the future, it looks to be an exclusionary one offered as a palliative to lost dreams of upward mobility. Where the vast, open spaces of mid-century offices served to dehumanize and objectify workers, exclusionary offices prey upon contemporary workers' feelings of inadequacy and their frustrations about the static nature of modern work. But we, the multitudinous descendants of Brother Dominic, don't have to take the bait. We don't *need* these spaces, even if we still want offices where we can connect and collaborate rather than simply hide behind our respective inboxes. We can do our work anywhere, as those who protested Starbucks' more inclusive corporate policies recently showed us, albeit somewhat ironically. We don't have to do it inside of gilded enclosures that milk our meager salaries for hundreds of dollars a month; we don't have to pay for the privilege of having friends or colleagues, and we should be wary of any and all arguments to the contrary.

If the history and culture of the office has taught us anything, it's that material trends come and go but that the social connections that manifest inside of the confines they create are real and can be long lasting, if we want them to be. The work of producing, maintaining, and managing information that was central to the rise of the knowledge economy in the twentieth century—and to the office, as well—will continue to draw humans together, forcing them to talk and interact in order to solve problems. What will change is how that interaction gets recognized, compensated and, perhaps, consecrated as well via physical space. The 2008 recession was felt hardest among the middle class, including white-collar office workers, and as the historian Sam Haselby points out, those office jobs probably aren't coming back. Ever. Part of that trend has to do with those machines we office workers have been tending, which are quickly becoming smart enough, thanks to our input and training, to tend to *us*. As Haselby explains, "economists who study employment trends tell us that almost half of existing jobs, including those involving 'non-routine cognitive tasks'—you know, like *thinking*—are at risk of death by computerization within 20 years."[24] Exclusive, members-only offices peddling needs-based upholstery and single origin coffee will not save any of us from what promises to be a whole suite of radical changes to the way we do and understand office work. What they may do, for a little while, anyway, is offer aesthetically pleasing insulation to absorb the shocks that we workers will be made to personally feel, having been trained for generations to tie our self-worth to our jobs and, by extension, to our offices.

The end of the office, I would like to suggest at the last, has already arrived and brought with it plenty of discomfort, but likewise opportunity. If we cannot rely on offices to nourish and shape the identities of white-collar workers, or "creative" workers, or to lend dignity to any of the work that those people do, then we are free to create those definitions for ourselves under alternative constraints and outside of the realm of work. I do not deny the difficulty of doing so, since the work that one does and the environment in which one does it has provided a fundamental means of sifting and sorting the population and, thus, of asserting one's own place in it for hundreds of years. But if we take to heart some very old ideas about the meaning of work—namely, Marx's observation that central to the idea of *value* itself is "socially necessary labor time"[25]—and put them to use in the context of this new and somewhat confusing landscape of creative production, we might arrive somewhere different in our thinking about what it was that we were doing for all those years when we were working inside our offices. Because we weren't just producing and managing information or creating documents; we were producing something much more important, a social context for living *and* working, formed through exchange and interaction. It's the only thing that really matters, in the end. Offices helped us to do it, once, and if they don't anymore, it's time for us to decide what else will.

ACKNOWLEDGMENTS

've had a lot of conversations with a lot of people about a lot of offices, and I'm grateful for every single one of them.

My first thank-yous go to my parents, Jim and Sandra Liming, who first allowed me to visit their offices long ago in the spirit of Take Your Daughter to Work Day. Right behind them are the many supportive officemates I've had over the years—particularly back in graduate school, when sharing an office meant living in pretty close quarters. My thanks to Necia Werner, Robert Kilpatrick, and Dan Markowicz (plus Bozo), for being so easy to live with. I'd also like to thank Kristin Ellwanger and Cheryl Misialek, the administrative staff in the English Department at the University of North Dakota, who help to keep our big, collective office running smoothly.

Much of my research wouldn't have been possible without the support and suggestions of colleagues like Matt Bucher (who visited the Ransom Center when I myself could not), and Daniel Hefko and Paul Devlin, who shared resources and materials with me. Ian Petrie gave me lots of great ideas that I didn't have time to follow up on, and countless others on Twitter talked me down from an assortment of intellectual ledges, for which I am also grateful. Thank you, too, to Al Muchka and the Milwaukee Public Museum for letting me spend time with the wonderful objects in the Dietz Collection. Thank you to Ira Gerlich, who was kind enough to show me around The Spheres at Amazon, and to my friends Michael Berger and Ronny Ewanek, who gave me a tour of the Basecamp offices and also of the Soho House in Chicago. Thanks to Lee Konstantinou for editing the piece on The Spheres that appeared in the *Los Angeles Review of Books* and was duly improved as a result. Thanks to the students in the English 408: Writing for Digital Environments class that met during the spring of 2019 who voted on cover designs, and to Alice Marwick for doing such a smashing job with it. As series editors, Chris Schaberg and Ian Bogost have been incredibly supportive, and Haaris Naqvi and Amy Martin at Bloomsbury have done a wonderful job of overseeing the whole publication process.

As my first thank-yous are to my family, my final thank-yous are to Dave and Meriwether, my adopted family members, who I love and adore and with whom I am privileged share my other office, our home.

NOTES

Introduction

1 Volker Hartkopf, quoted in Alan Boyle, "Futuristic office space hides the high tech," NBC News, November 10, 2005, http://www.nbcnews.com/id/9972711/ns/technology_and_science-innovation/t/futuristic-office-space-hides-high-tech/#.XV2Ls FB7mso.

2 Upton Sinclair, *The Brass Check: A Study of American Journalism* (Champaign, IL: University of Illinois Press, 2003), 77–8.

3 Niraj Chokshi, "Out of the Office: More People Are Working Remotely, Survey Finds," *New York Times*, February 15, 2017, https://www.nytimes.com/2017/02/15/us/remote-workers-wo rk-from-home.html.

4 Jessica Guynn, "Yahoo CEO Marissa Mayer causes uproar with telecommuting ban," *Los Angeles Times*, February 26, 2013, https://www.latimes.com/business/la-xpm-2013-feb-26-la-fi-ya hoo-telecommuting-20130226-story.html.

5 Jene Barr and Charles Lynch III, *Busy Office, Busy People* (Chicago: A. Whitman and Company, 1968), 1, 4, 7.

6 Daniel Akst, "Automation Anxiety," *Wilson's Quarterly*, summer 2013, http://archive.wilsonquarterly.com/essays/automation-an xiety.

Chapter 1

1 Nikil Saval, *Cubed: A Secret History of the Workplace* (New York: Doubleday, 2014), 13.

2 Herman, *The Restoration of the Monastery at St. Martin of Tournai*, tr. Lynn H. Nelson (Washington, DC: Catholic University of America Press, 1996), 114.

3 Xerox Corporation, "It's a Miracle!" television commercial, July 1975, https://www.youtube.com/watch?v=LAt-lB9JIqw.

4 Saval, *Cubed*, 9.

5 Ralph Waldo Emerson, *Essays* (New York: Bay View Publishing, 1860), 35.

6 Nathaniel Hawthorne, *The Scarlet Letter* (New York: Norton, 2005), 9.

7 Herman Melville, "Bartleby, the Scrivener," *Norton Introduction to Literature*, ed. Mays (New York: Norton, 2016), 664.

8 Melville, "Bartleby," 665, 667.

9 Benjamin Kline Hunnicutt, *Free Time* (Philadelphia: Temple University Press, 2013), vii.

10 Elizabeth Gaskell, *North and South* (London: Smith, Elder, and Company, 1900), 107.

11 National Fire Insurance Company, *A Quarter-Century's Fire Underwriting, 1871–1896: An Historical and Biographical Milestone in the Life of the National Fire Insurance Co. of Hartford, Conn.* (New York: The DeVinne Press, 1897), 130.

12 Ibid., 129, 131.

13 Sarah Grand, "The New Aspect of the Woman Question," *North American Review* 158, no. 448 (March 1894): 276.

14 Carol Srole, *Masculinity and Femininity in Nineteenth-Century Courts and Offices* (Ann Arbor: University of Michigan Press, 2010), 162.

15 "Pilot," *The Office*, dir. Ken Kwapis. NBC, March 24, 2005.

16 Sinclair Lewis, *Babbitt* (New York: Signet Classics, 1991), 31–34, 170.

17 Frederick Winslow Taylor, *The Principles of Scientific Management* (New York: Harper and Brothers, 1913), 13.

18 Hunnicutt, *Free Time*, 113.

19 SC Johnson and Son, Inc., "The Frank Lloyd Wright Buildings at SC Johnson," http://www.scjohnson.com/en/company/arch itecture/Wright-Buildings.aspx

20 Saval, *Cubed*, 65–9.

21 Lewis Mumford, *The Culture of Cities* (New York: Harvest / HBJ Publishers, 1970), 410.

22 Frank Lloyd Wright, interview with Mike Wallace, September 28, 1957, The Harry Ransom Center, University of Texas, http://www.hrc.utexas.edu/multimedia/video/2008/wallace/wrig ht_frank_lloyd_t.html.

23 Frank Lloyd Wright Foundation. "SC Johnson Drawings," PBS.org, http://www.pbs.org/flw/buildings/scjohnson/scjohns on_drawings.html.

24 Patrick Sisson, "Frank Lloyd's Visionary SC Johnson Buildings, 'The Shape of Things to Come,'" *Curbed*, October 5, 2015, https://www.curbed.com/2015/10/5/9914538/frank-llo yd-wright-sc-johnson-administration-building.

25 "PPG Pittsburgh Paints Cherokee Red," Encycolorpedia.com, http://encycolorpedia.com/79413a.

26 "SC Johnson Headquarters—Detail of The Great Workroom," silver gelatin photo, 1939, photographer unknown, in Jonathan Lipman, *Frank Lloyd Wright and the Johnson Wax Building* (New York: Rizzoli International Publications, 1986), 102.

Chapter 2

1 An 1895 patent for a "Receptacle for letters or other papers" designed by William A. Cooke Jr. offers some insight into the history of the filing cabinet. Previously, paper bundles would have been stored in pigeon-hole style shelving lining the walls of an office space. Cooke's design, by contrast, is for a "compartmented box receptacle for letters and other papers which when placed in position and its fastening released shall be adapted to automatically unclose and in the act simultaneously spread apart" granting "free and ready access to any or all of the compartments is secured." See William A. Cooke Jr., "US533053: Receptacle for letters or other papers," January 29, 1895, Google Patents, https://patents.google.com/patent/US533053.

2 Tess Slesinger, *The Unpossessed* (New York: New York Review Books, 2002), 28–9.

3 Ibid., 30.

4 Alexandra Lange, "White-Collar Corbusier: From the *Casier* to the *Cités d'Affaires*," *Grey Room* 9 (2002): 65.

5 Ibid., 74, emphasis original.

6 Esther Kihn Beamer, *Effective Secretarial Practices* (Cincinnati, OH: South-Western Publishing Company, 1949), 26, https://archive.org/details/effectivesecreta00beam.

7 John William Schulze, *The American Office: Its Organization, Management, and Records* (New York: The Ronald Press Company, 1913), https://archive.org/details/americanofficeit00schurich.

8 Ibid., 38.

9 Saval styles Robert Probst, the man behind the "Action Office" designs of the 1960s, as the "inventor" of the cubicle, even though historical documents and photographs show versions of them dating from the early 1900s. Saval, though, is right to credit Probst as the inventor of the *contemporary* cubicle, which debuted in 1968 and grew in popularity throughout the 1970s and 1980s. See Saval, *Cubed*, 6, 216–20, and "A Brief History of the Dreaded Office Cubicle," *Wall Street Journal*, May 9, 2014, https://www.wsj.com/articles/a-brief-history-of-the-dreaded-office-cubicle-1399681972.

10 Richard Yates, *Revolutionary Road* (New York: Vintage, 2008), 128.

11 Saval, "A Brief History of the Dreaded Cubicle."

12 Sophie Treadwell, *Machinal* (London: Nick Hern Books, 2017).

13 Schulze, *The American* Office, 27–8.

14 Ibid., 28.

15 The Rank Organisation, "Look at Life—Rising to the High Office," narr. by Tim Turner, 1963, accessed June 19, 2019, https://youtu.be/8zUQD1p9bXY.

16 Mills popularized the term "white collar," following Upton Sinclair's original use of it, with reference to the group of "gratifyingly middle class" workers who populated both offices and the established professions (like medicine and law) in mid-century America. See C. Wright Mills, *White Collar* (Oxford: Oxford University Press, 1951).

17 Saval, *Cubed*, 193.

18 *Office Space*, dir. Mike Judge, 20th Century Fox, 1999.

19 Julie Lasky, "Designing Distraction: Executive Toys," *New York Times*, February 4, 2015, accessed June 19, 2019, https://www.nytimes.com/2015/02/05/garden/

designing-distraction-executive-toys.html.

20 Gertrude Stein, *Everybody's Autobiography* (New York: Vintage, 1973), 73.

21 Ronald Goodrich quoted in Susan S. Szenasy, *Private and Executive Offices* (New York: Facts on File, 1984), 8.

22 Quoted in Laski, "Designing Distraction."

23 Bryce Covert, "Americans Work Too Much Already," *Nation*, September 28, 2018, accessed June 19, 2019, https://www.thenation.com/article/americans-work-too-much-already/.

24 *Fight Club*, dir. David Fincher, Fox Searchlight Productions, 1999.

25 Thomas A. Russo, "Thomas A. Russo Museum of Business History and Technology," YouTube, uploaded by the Business Technology Association, February 3, 2016, https://www.youtube.com/watch?v=Ni3QVWw1k8c.

26 Milwaukee Public Museum, "Dietz Typewriter Collection," accessed July 3, 2019, http://archive.mpm.edu/research-collections/history/online-collections-research/dietz-typewriter-collection.

Chapter 3

1 Henri Lefebvre, *The Production of Space*, tr. Donald Nicholson-Smith (New York: Blackwell, 1991), 98.

2 Yates, *Revolutionary Road*, 74.

3 *The Hudsucker Proxy*, dir. Ethan Coen and Joel Coen, Warner Bros., 1994.

4 Kenneth Fearing, *The Big Clock* (New York: New York Review Books, 2006), 27.

5 Ibid., 175.

6 *The Hudsucker Proxy*.

7 Harvey observes that, given the "growing abstractions of space" experienced during the late nineteenth and early twentieth centuries, architects like Louis Henry Sullivan looked to harness and, to a certain extent, *establish* recognizable "vernacular" styles of architecture in America. The skyscraper was a unique American invention that succeeded in doing that. See David Harvey, *The Condition of Post-Modernity* (New York: Blackwell, 1989), 272.

8 Keith Payne, *The Broken Ladder: How Inequality Affects the Way We Live, Think, and Die* (New York: Penguin, 2017), 181.

9 Larry Ross, quoted in Studs Terkel, *Working* (New York: The New Press, 2004), 406–7.

10 Rem Koolhaas, *Delirious New York* (New York: Monacelli, 1994), 82.

11 *30 Rock*, "Sandwich Day," Season 2, Episode 14, May 1, 2008.

12 Koolhaas, *Delirious New York*, 88.

13 John Hartford, "In Tall Buildings," *Nobody Knows What You Do*, Flying Fish Records, 1976.

14 Yates, *Revolutionary Road*, 125–6.

15 Adrienne Brown, *The Black Skyscraper: Architecture and the Perception of Race* (Baltimore, MD: Johns Hopkins University Press, 2017), 2.

16 *Mad Men*, "The Wheel," Season 1, Episode 13, October 18, 2007.

17 Virginia Woolf, *A Room of One's Own* (New York: Harcourt: 1981), 108.

18 *Mad Men*, "The Mountain King," Season 2, Episode 12, October 18, 2008.

19 Woolf, *A Room of One's Own*, 4.

20 Christopher Ingraham, "The American Commute is Worse Than It's Ever Been," *Washington Post*, February 22, 2017, https://www.washingtonpost.com/news/wonk/wp/2017/0 2/22/the-american-commute-is-worse-today-than-its- ever_ been/?noredirect=on&utm_term=.d31ea243ba52.

21 Andrea Komlosy, *Work: The Last 1,000 Years*, tr. Jacob K. Watson and Loren Balhorn (New York: Verso, 2018), 184.

22 *Desk Set*, dir. Walter Lang, 20th Century Fox, 1957.

23 *Mad Men*, "Christmas Comes but Once a Year," Season 4, Episode 2, August 1, 2010.

24 Friedrich Engels, *The Origin of the Family, Private Property, and the State* (New York: International Publishers, 1942), 58.

25 *The Mary Tyler Moore Show*, "Christmas and the Hard-Luck Kid II," Season 1, Episode 14, December 19, 1970.

26 See Louis Hyman, *Temp: How American Work, American Business, and the American Dream Became Temporary* (New York: Viking, 2018), 36–41, 51–3.

27 Halle Butler, *The New Me* (New York: Penguin, 2019), 159.

28 Ibid., 77, emphasis added.

29 Jay Yarrow, "Amazon Has a Brutal System for Employees Trying to Get Promoted," *Business Insider*, October 16, 2013, https://www.businessinsider.com/amazons-brutal-promotio n-system-2013-10.

30 This statistic is included in a report published by the
MacArthur Foundation about the risings cost of housing and
its effects on the economic prospects of younger workers. See
MacArthur Foundation, "How Housing Matters," MacFound.
org, May 15, 2015, https://www.macfound.org/media/files/
E11540_How_Housing_Matters_FULLREPORT.pdf.

Chapter 4

1 See, for example, Alison Coleman, "Is Google's model of the
creative workplace the future of the office?," *The Guardian*,
February 11, 2016, https://www.theguardian.com/careers
/2016/feb/11/is-googles-model-of-the-creative-workplace
-the-future-of-the-office.

2 Andrew Ross, *No Collar: The Humane Workplace and Its
Hidden Costs* (Philadelphia: Temple University Press, 2004),
253.

3 Tina Bringslimark, Terry Hartig, and Grete Patil,
"Psychological Benefits of Indoor Plants in Workplaces:
Putting Experimental Results into Context," *HortScience: a
publication of the American Society for Horticultural Science*
42.3, June 2007, http://dx.doi.org/10.21273/HORTSCI.42.3.
581.

4 Edmond O. Wilson, *Biophilia* (Cambridge, MA: Harvard
University Press, 1984), 2.

5 Erich Fromm, "The Necrophilous Character," in *The Erich
Fromm Reader: Readings Selected and Edited by Rainer Funk*
(Westminster, MD: Promethus, 1994), 124.

6 Amazon.com, "Inspiring innovation with Biophilia,"
DayOne—the Amazon blog, November 20, 2017, https://bl

og.aboutamazon.com/amazon-offices/inspiring-innovation-with-biophilia.

7   Douglas Spencer, *The Architecture of Neoliberalism* (New York: Bloomsbury, 2016), 7.

8   Ibid., 46.

9   Ibid., 16.

10 Charles Mudede, "The New Seattle and the Amazon Spheres," *The Stranger*, January 29, 2018, https://www.thestranger.com/slog/2018/01/29/25761009/the-new-seattle-and-the-bezos-spheres.

11 Seth King, quoted in Chavie Lieber, "Amazon employees are using Prime Day to push for better working conditions," Vox.com, July 16, 2018, https://www.vox.com/2018/7/16/17577614/amazon-prime-day-strike-boycotts.

12 Kaitlyn Tiffany, "What you see on Amazon's public warehouse tours," Vox.com, June 26, 2019, https://www.vox.com/the-goods/2019/6/26/18758599/amazon-fulfillment-center-tour-robots-workers.

13 "Soho House Chicago—Membership," SohoHouseChicago.com, 2019, https://www.sohohousechicago.com/membership.

14 Ibid.

15 Jennifer Gould Keil, "Posh Soho House Boots 'Uncool' Members," *New York Post*, March 1, 2010, https://nypost.com/2010/03/01/posh-soho-house-boots-uncool-members/.

16 "The Wing—Who We Are," TheWing.com, 2019, https://www.the-wing.com/who-we-are/.

17 "The Wing—Why the Wing," TheWing.com, 2019, https://www.the-wing.com/why-the-wing/.

18 Amanda Arnold, "The Wing Is Under Investigation by the New York Human Rights Commission," *The Cut*, March 27, 2018, https://www.thecut.com/2018/03/the-wing-discrimina tion-investigation-human-rights-commission.html. See also the follow-up by Lisa Ryan, "Co-Working Space The Wing Is No Longer Just For Women," *The Cut*, January 4, 2019, https:// www.thecut.com/2019/01/the-wing-membership-policy-mo re-inclusive.html.

19 Kara Cuttruzzula. "Why are 8,000 Women on This Club's Waitlist?" *The Bridge*, July 25, 2017, https://thebridgebk.com/ why-this-women-only-club-is-a-perfect-fit-for-brooklyn/.

20 Mimi Montgomery, "I Got Into The Wing in D.C. Here's Why I Can't Join," *Washingtonian*, April 12, 2018, https://www.was hingtonian.com/2018/04/12/i-got-into-the-wing-in-dc-her es-why-i-cant-join/.

21 Quoted in Juliette Garside, "Many more of us will work from home—or a café—says BT futurologist," *The Guardian*, January 2, 2014, https://www.theguardian.com/money/2014/j an/02/working-from-home-communications-technology-bt-futurologist.

22 Daniel Henninger, "Starbucks' Homeless Problem" *Wall Street Journal*, May 23, 2018, https://www.wsj.com/articles/starbu cks-homeless-problem-1527114340.

23 "Deplorable EricD" @TheMotleyMind, "Goodbye, @Starbucks," May 29, 2018, 7:27 a.m. tweet, https://twitter.com/ starbucksnews/status/1001418832307630080?lang=en.

24 Sam Haselby, "Fuck Work," *Aeon*, November 25, 2016, https://aeon.co/essays/what-if-jobs-are-not-the-solution-but -the-problem.

25 Marx uses the word "congealed" to show how socially determined estimations of worthwhile labor appear latent in the "value" of a particular commodity. David Harvey translates this idea as "socially necessary labor time," a phrase which he uses in his video lectures on Marx. See Karl Marx, *Capital, Vol. I*, tr. Fowkes (New York: Penguin, 1990), 128; and David Harvey, "Reading Marx's *Capital, Vol. I*—Class 1, Introduction," DavidHarvey.org, June 12, 2008, http://davidharvey.org/2008/06/marxs-capital-class-01/.

INDEX

Page references for illustrations appear in *italics*.